John Locke, John Edward Russell

The Philosophy of Locke

In Extracts from the Essay Concerning Human Understanding

John Locke, John Edward Russell

The Philosophy of Locke
In Extracts from the Essay Concerning Human Understanding

ISBN/EAN: 9783337077501

Printed in Europe, USA, Canada, Australia, Japan

Cover: Foto ©Thomas Meinert / pixelio.de

More available books at **www.hansebooks.com**

Series of Modern Philosophers
Edited by E. Hershey Sneath, Ph.D.

THE
PHILOSOPHY OF LOCKE

IN EXTRACTS FROM

THE ESSAY
CONCERNING HUMAN UNDERSTANDING

ARRANGED, WITH INTRODUCTORY NOTES,

BY

JOHN E. RUSSELL, A.M.
Mark Hopkins Professor of Philosophy in Williams College

NEW YORK
HENRY HOLT AND COMPANY
1891

EDITOR'S PROSPECTUS.

THIS book, containing extracts from the Philosophy of Locke, is the first of a series to be published under my editorial supervision, for the purpose of presenting the substance of the representative systems of modern philosophy in selections from the original works. Each volume is to be prefaced by a short biographical sketch of the author, a statement of the historical position of the system, a brief exposition of the system, and a bibliography.

Eight volumes have been arranged for, as follows: Des Cartes, by Professor Torrey, of the University of Vermont; Spinoza, by Professor Fullerton, of the University of Pennsylvania; Locke, by Professor Russell, of Williams College; Berkeley, by ex-President Porter, of Yale University; Hume, by Professor Aikins, of Trinity College, N. C.; Reid, by the editor of the series; Kant, by Professor Watson, of Queen's University, Canada;* Hegel, by Professor Royce, of Harvard University. If sufficient encouragement is given, volumes representing Leibnitz, Jacobi, Fichte, Herbart, Schelling, Schopenhauer, Hartmann, and Spencer will probably follow.

* The publishers have purchased an edition of Professor Watson's excellent book, entitled "Extracts from the Philosophy of Kant," and include it in this series.

iii

The object of the series is primarily to facilitate the study of the history of philosophy in our colleges.. In many colleges that course is gradually being enlarged, and a mere text-book on the subject is inadequate to meet the wants of the department. One simply furnishes a brief exposition of the various systems, which, it must be remembered, is merely an *interpretation*. It is especially desirable, however, to put the student *in direct contact with the text of the author*, permitting him to make his own interpretation. This cannot be done by resorting to the complete works of the various authors, because, if a number of systems is to be studied, in the majority of cases the books are too elaborate, and, in German Philosophy, too expensive. This series provides for this difficulty by giving the substance of each system in selections from the author's works, and in a form involving little expense on the part of the student.

A secondary object of the series is to meet the wants of a large number of professional men, especially clergymen, who are desirous of a wider acquaintance with philosophy ; but, not having time to read the complete works, still desire something more than a brief interpretation—such as may be found in works on the History of Philosophy.

E. HERSHEY SNEATH.

YALE UNIVERSITY, *October*, 1891.

BIOGRAPHICAL SKETCH.

JOHN LOCKE was born at Wrington, a village in Somersetshire, August 29, 1632; and he died at Oates, in Essex, a town about twenty miles from London, October 28, 1704. His life period, seventy-two years, coincided with one of the stormiest and most eventful epochs in the political and religious history of England, and in the most important movements of this epoch Locke had an influential part.

Of Locke's ancestors we have little certain information. His father claimed a sort of cousinship with one John Locke, who was mayor of Bristol in 1642, and who was descended from an earlier John Locke, a sheriff of London in 1460. Our John Locke's great-grandfather was Edward Locke, a younger member of a branch that had settled in Dorsetshire in the sixteenth century.

Locke's mother, it is probable, died when he was very young. The only positive information we have about her from Locke himself is a single sentence of Lady Masham's, "What I remember him to have said of his mother expressed her to be a very pious woman and affectionate mother." Of his father Locke has given quite explicit information; and it was doubtless to him that Locke was most indebted for the favoring circumstances of his early life, and Locke speaks of him with the warmest appreciation and respect. Lady Masham says, "From Mr. Locke I have often heard of his father that he was a man of parts. Mr. Locke never mentioned him but with great respect and affection." Locke's father was an attorney, and appears to have had a successful practice until the breaking out of the civil war terminated his peaceful career. He joined the cause of the Parliament, and served as captain under his friend and legal associate, Alexander Popham, who held the rank of colonel. The civil war nearly ruined Locke's father financially, though he retrieved his fortunes in a considerable degree, and at his death in 1661 he left a comfortable estate to his two sons. The older son, Thomas, dying shortly after his father, John Locke was left in sole possession of the family estate.

Locke's student life began at Westminster School, then under the charge of the famous Dr. Busby. Locke was admitted to this school as a king's scholar, through the influence of Colonel Popham, in 1646, and here he remained probably six years, when he entered Christ's College, Oxford, as Westminster student. His matriculation bears the date of November 27, 1652, and he began his residence in the Michaelmas term, December 22 of the same year.

Locke's connection with Oxford continued for thirty-two years, though his residence there was confined for the most part to the ten years following his matriculation. He received his Bachelor's degree in 1656, his Master's degree in 1658. In 1660 he was made Greek Lecturer; Rhetorical Reader in 1663; and Censor of Moral Science in 1664. These, with the senior studentship at Christ's College, were the only academic positions that Locke held.

In 1666 Locke appears to have made his final decision not to take orders, as his father had designed; he chose medicine, and, though he should properly have forfeited his studentship,—that being an ecclesiastical one,—by a royal dispensation, which is still preserved and bears the date of November 14, 1666, he was permitted to retain the senior studentship in Christ's College, and this fellowship he continued to hold until his expulsion from Oxford by the mandate of Charles II. in 1684.

Oxford, when Locke entered it, was under Puritan control. Cromwell was chancellor; Dr. John Owen, the most distinguished Independent, was vice-chancellor and dean of Christ Church. During the civil wars the university had suffered greatly; its discipline had been greatly relaxed, and general disorder prevailed, but at the time when Locke was a student there the discipline of the university had been much improved,—the university was suffering, in fact, from the opposite extreme,—the closest religious censorship was exercised over the students; to quote from the records of the time—"frequent preaching in every house was the chief matter aimed at. In June, 1653, it was ordered that all Bachelors of Arts and undergraduates in colleges and in halls be required, every Lord's Day, to give an account, to some person of known ability and piety, of the sermons they had heard, and their attendance on other religious exercises on that day." Nor were such exercises limited to Sundays; in most, if not all the colleges, two or more such services were held during the week, at which all members of the university were required to be present. Such rigorous and narrow discipline was doubtless irksome to such a nature as Locke's, but he nowhere speaks of it with dissatisfaction. The influence, however, which he *did* deprecate, and from which his mind reacted strongly, was the scholastic form of teaching then prevalent at Oxford.

Lady Masham says: "I have often heard him say, in reference to his first years spent in the university, that he had so small satisfaction there from his studies, as finding very little light there brought to his understanding—that he became discontented with his manner of life, and wished his father had rather designed him for anything else that what he was destined to. This discouragement kept him from being a very hard student."

It would hardly be correct to conclude, even from Locke's own statements, that he derived from these earlier years at Oxford no really important benefit; even the scholastic training was not without a strong and permanent influence upon Locke's mental development, as is evinced in his chief work, the "Essay Concerning Human Understanding"—a book that would hardly have been written if he had not passed such years at Oxford.

5. There were two influences which later in Locke's student-life at Oxford contributed powerfully to mould the development of his mind and to determine the direction of his life; one of these influences was that of the new philosophy of free inquiry determined by experience. This influence sprung both from Des Cartes and Bacon, and reached Locke indirectly, but which, according to his testimony, awakened him to

new life. It was, however, to Des Cartes rather than to his English predecessors, Bacon and Hobbes, that Locke was the more indebted for this early quickening and direction of his mind. "He often told me," says Lady Masham, "that the first books that gave him a relish for philosophical reading were those of Des Cartes."

The other strong influence upon Locke at this time was a religious one, and came from his intimate association with the dean of his college, Dr. John Owen. Locke's debt to this large and liberal mind is a large one; he learned from him to take liberal and tolerant views of religious differences; the doctrine of toleration, which Locke so profoundly taught and illustrated, had its inception in no slight degree from the influence of John Owen.

The year 1666 marks a turning-point in the career of Locke. In the autumn of the previous year he had, as secretary, accompanied Sir Walter Vane, who had been sent on an embassy to the Elector of Brandenburg. On his return, in the spring of 1666, Locke was tendered the post of secretary to the Earl of Sandwich, then about to set out for Spain as embassador. This offer, after considerable hesitation, he declined, remarking that he may "have let slip the minute that they say every man has once in his life to make himself."

In the same year Locke met for the first time, and became the friend of, Lord Ashley, afterwards the Earl of Shaftesbury, and the most powerful nobleman of his time. This acquaintance with Lord Ashley, due to the most casual circumstance, was of decisive import to Locke's subsequent life; almost with the beginning of this connection, Locke entered upon a new career, and began to participate in and to influence public affairs. In the following year he became a member of Lord Ashley's family, and from that time he shared the varying fortunes of his patron. In the household of Lord Ashley, Locke appears to have discharged miscellaneous duties; he was medical adviser, tutor to Ashley's son, and secretary and confidential adviser to Lord Ashley.

Locke's circumstances at this time were happy and favorable to his chosen pursuits. Outside of Ashley's family he practised medicine but little, but he had leisure for study, and opportunities for acquaintance with the most distinguished men in learning and in public life. In 1668 Locke was elected a Fellow of the Royal Society, which had been founded not long before by Boyle. In 1669 and in 1672 he was a member of a council belonging to this society, but he never took an active part in the proceedings of the society.

In 1672 Lord Ashley was created Earl of Shaftesbury, and a little later he was appointed Lord Chancellor of England. Locke was then made Secretary of Presentations, with a salary of three hundred pounds. He had previously, in 1667, been made, in an informal way, chief secretary and manager of the Company known as Lords Proprietors of Carolina. This informal but onerous office he held till the autumn of 1672, and in the discharge of his multifarious duties he evinced those talents and versatility of powers that so distinguished him in later years.

In November, 1673, Shaftesbury incurred the king's displeasure and was dismissed from office, and Locke lost his secretaryship. He had, however, been appointed secretary for the Council of Trade, with a salary of five hundred pounds, and this office he continued to hold until the dissolution of the council in March, 1674, though in fact the salary was never paid.

In 1674-5 Locke received the degree of Bachelor of Medicine, and in the January following he was appointed to one of the two medical studentships in Christ's College. The income from this studentship, together with an annuity of one hundred pounds granted him by Shaftesbury, and the revenue from his small estates in Somersetshire, secured to him a comfortable maintenance.

One circumstance belonging to this period, from its connection with Locke's philosophical career, should not be passed over; it was the historical occasion of the "Essay Concerning Human Understanding," spoken of by him in the Epistle to the Reader. This memorable meeting occurred probably in 1670-71.

In 1675 Locke's health, which had been precarious for some time, was now so seriously impaired that he resolved to make a sojourn in France. He left England the same year, and on Christmas Day he reached Montpellier, the place he had selected for his residence, and there he remained for the most of the time till the spring of 1677.

The chief occupation of Locke during the period of his residence in France was the Essay, the few scattered notes for which he had prepared in England. It is probable that before he returned to England, in

1679, he had advanced the work upon the Essay well toward its completion. In a letter to Thonyard, in 1679, he speaks of the work as "completed," adding that "he thought too well of it to let it go from his hands."

Locke returned to London on April 30, 1679, to find Shaftesbury again in royal favor and president of the newly formed council. Shaftesbury had need of Locke's services only for a short time; he was soon in opposition again, and his tenure of office quickly came to an end.

Shaftesbury's political career was soon terminated. In July, 1681, he was arrested on a charge of high treason and confined in the Tower; he was indicted by a special commission, November 24th, but on December 1st the Grand Jury threw out the bill, and Shaftesbury was acquitted, but only to enjoy a brief triumph. In the spring of 1682-3 he was implicated in a scheme to effect a general uprising against the king; the scheme failed, and Shaftesbury for safety took refuge in Holland, where he died in January, 1683. Shaftesbury's fall rendered Locke's situation unpleasant and somewhat dangerous; and, though there was no evidence to implicate him in Shaftesbury's designs, he was suspected and watched. Partly for this reason and partly on account of his disgust at the turn affairs were taking in England, he determined upon what he regarded as voluntary exile. He left England some time in 1683, and arrived in Holland late in the same year.

The five years Locke passed in Holland, though not the happiest, were probably the most favorable to his aims and the most fruitful of results of any period in his lifetime. In these years he matured the preparation of his most important works, and it was in Holland that he began to give to the world the fruit of his many years of profound study and wide experience; it was in Holland that he formed some of the friendships he valued most highly,—with Limborch, the distinguished theologian of the Remonstrants, and with whom he maintained the closest and most affectionate intercourse during the remainder of his life; and also with Le Clerc, whose acquaintance he formed in 1685-6, and to whom Locke was indebted for the first distinctive impulse to authorship. Le Clerc was just projecting the "Bibliothèque Universelle," and by his instigation Locke published in this periodical the epitome of the "Essay Concerning Human Understanding" in 1688.

During his stay in Holland Locke had no permanent residence; he resided principally in Amsterdam, Utrecht, and Rotterdam. The winter of 1683-4 he probably passed in Amsterdam. In 1684 he made a tour through Holland, and he appears to have returned to Amsterdam the following winter.

After the death of Charles II. in February, 1684-5, Locke, being suspected of complicity in the attempt to set the Duke of Monmouth on the English throne, was included among those persons deemed dangerous and whom the government of Holland was requested to deliver up. Locke was compelled for a time to be in hiding and to assume a fictitious name. He stayed for some time in the house of Dr. Veen, in Amsterdam, and as Dr. Van der Linden he made a brief sojourn in Cleves. This political danger, however, passed away in 1686.

The winter of 1686-7 was spent in Amsterdam, and after a brief sojourn at Utrecht in the following summer, Locke took up his residence with Mr. Benjamin Furly in Rotterdam, at whose house he continued to reside till the winter of 1687-8, and for whom he formed a strong personal attachment.

In November, 1688, William of Orange set out on his expedition to England. Locke followed in February of the next year, and on the 12th of February he was back in London, and at once he entered upon the most active and laborious periods of his life. Two positions were offered him by King William,—the post of ambassador to Frederick, the first Elector of Brandenburg, and a like position at the Court of Vienna. Locke declined both honors on the ground of poor health and unfitness for such responsibilities; but at his own suggestion he was made Commissioner of Appeals, an office which he retained during the remainder of his life.

The years that followed immediately upon Locke's return to England were crowded with arduous and responsible labors. It was the period of the publication of all his more important writings, and during these six years he took a most active interest in political affairs, and, directly or indirectly, did more, it is probable, to shape the policy of the new government than any single mind of his generation. His hand is traceable in the most important measures of William's government; his direct assistance or counsel was sought by the king himself or by his advisers on all matters of importance. The Toleration Bill, which effected important religious changes; the measure for reorganizing the currency and restoring a proper standard of value—perhaps the most important measure of William's reign—were largely Locke's work; and of the Board of Trade, which had in charge the economic and industrial interests of the country, Locke was for years the "presiding genius."

Locke's authorship during these years was prodigious. "The Essay Concerning Human Understanding" was published in 1690. "The Epistola Tolerantia" preceded it by a few months. The two treatises on Government appeared the same year. Two subsequent Letters on Toleration. A second and third edition of the Essay, and a number of lesser publications on economic subjects, and an "Essay on the Reasonableness of Christianity" were published during these years.

In 1700 Locke was compelled by feeble health to abandon all political service. He had some years before made his home in the family of Sir Francis and Lady Masham at their country seat at Oates, in Essex. Here Locke passed the closing years of his life, and these years were most happy and tranquil. The last important literary work of his was the publication of the fourth edition of the Essay, which appeared in 1700. Four years later, on October 28, Locke passed away, and his body was buried in the churchyard at High Laver.

THE PHILOSOPHY OF LOCKE, AND THE POSITION IT OCCUPIES IN THE HISTORY OF MODERN PHILOSOPHY.

The position which Locke occupies in the development of modern philosophy can be best determined by an examination of his chief philosophical work, "The Essay Concerning Human Understanding."

The design of the Essay, as Locke states it, is "To inquire into the original, certainty, and extent of human knowledge, together with the grounds and degrees of belief, opinion and assent," and the method Locke proposes is, "1st, to inquire into the original of these ideas, notions, or whatever else you please to call them, which a man observes and is conscious to himself he has in his mind, and the ways whereby the understanding comes to be furnished with them; 2d, to show what knowledge the understanding hath by those ideas, and the certainty, evidence and extent of it."

Accordingly the Essay falls into two natural divisions, the first three books making the first division, and Book IV. constituting the second division. Locke's theory of knowledge is contained essentially in Books II. and IV., Book I. being hardly more than a negative answer to the fundamental question of Book II.; and Book III., in relation to the main design of the Essay, is an explanation of Book II.

Locke's theory of knowledge may be comprehended in the answer to two questions: 1st. How does the individual mind come to have knowledge? and 2d. What certain and real knowledge is possible to the individual mind? or, put more simply, What is it that the mind does in knowing, and consequently, What is it that the mind can certainly know?

Following now Locke's method, namely, "looking into one's own understanding to see how it works," we may epitomize Locke's account of human knowledge in this way: If I look into my mind to see what it is that I do in knowing, or how my knowledge comes to me, I find, first, that all knowledge consists in the perception of the agreement or disagreement of ideas,—ideas being whatever object the mind has immediately before it when it thinks or feels or wills; when, therefore, I analyze any act of knowledge, or any knowledge I am supposed to possess, I reach those simple elements of meaning which are not capable of further analysis; these are what I mean by simple ideas as the beginnings and materials of knowledge.

My first inquiry is, therefore, How do we come by these ideas; that is, How does there come to be meaning for my understanding? I answer: These elements of all possible knowledge come from experience and from experience only; they are not *innate;* by which I mean the mind is not in actual possession of any of them at our birth, but acquires them subsequently.

I do not deny that the mind has certain powers proper to it, and that it exerts them in the formation of knowledge nay, in the having of its simple ideas; I mean only that, prior to the awakening of the mind by the action of things upon the senses, there are no ideas in the understanding. Knowledge in a temporal respect begins with sensation. This experience, which is the source and beginning of knowledge, is of two kinds, external and internal; external experience is sensation, by which I mean "such an impression or motion made in some part of the body as produces some perception in the understanding;" internal experience is reflection, by which term I mean "that *notice* the mind takes of its own states and operations, by which it has ideas of the same."

Now since in the order of time external experience comes first, the proposition is true that ideas are coeval with sensation. But experience is not only the origin in time of knowledge; I find I am absolutely dependent upon experience for the kind of ideas I can have and the manner in which I have them. Simple ideas are the data for knowledge; in respect to these data my mind is passive and receptive rather than spontaneous and originative; I cannot create these single ideas at will; I am bound to have them, and to have them as they are determined by my experience; and in relation to that experience my mind is a *tabula rasa* upon which there can be no characters until there is the action of something upon it, or like a cabinet that remains dark until, through the openings in it, light is admitted and the reflection of objects is made within it. On the other hand, in the formation of complex ideas—they being those ideas that are made by modifying or compounding simple ideas in various ways—my mind is relatively free and originative; it can even proceed arbitrarily, since there need be no conformity of such ideas to the nature of objects extrinsic to the mind; but with ~~single~~ *simple* ideas such conformity or correspondence exists necessarily; and hence all simple ideas are true and adequate, while complex ideas may be, but are not necessarily, true or adequate.

Knowledge, as we have seen, consisting in the connection of ideas, depends for its certainty and extent upon the clearness, truth, and adequacy of our ideas. Knowledge can extend no further than we have ideas, and no further than we can perceive the relations between ideas. Knowledge is certain when that connection of ideas is clearly and certainly perceived, and knowledge is both certain and *real* when, as in the case of material objects, there is both the idea in our mind and the assurance or certainty that something doth exist to which the idea in some way corresponds. This assurance or conviction, though it is not knowledge in the strict sense of the definition, as it is more than belief or probability, may be included *in* knowledge. We have accordingly three degrees of knowledge: 1. Intuitive knowledge, where the connection between ideas is immediately and necessarily perceived. 2. Demonstrative knowledge, where the connection of ideas is certain, but is perceived indirectly by means of an intermediate idea. And 3. Sensitive knowledge, being the assurance or perfect conviction we have that some object extrinsic to the mind actually exists when we have the idea of such an object as has existed at those times when we had such ideas in the past.

Again, knowledge in respect to its possible objects is of three sorts : 1, of identity or diversity : 2, of co-existence and of other relations ; 3, of real existence. But these objects of knowledge reduce to two classes abstract ideas and matters of fact.

To the knowledge relating to ideas merely belong all abstract thinking and such sciences as logic and mathematics, since mathematics concerns things only so far as they conform to our ideas. To the knowledge of matters of fact belong, 1, the knowledge of existences, our own existence, which we know by intuition, and the existence of God, which we know by demonstration, and the existence of external objects, which we know by the testimony of our senses and by our memory. To this class of knowable objects belong, 2, the knowledge of the co-existence of qualities in objects perceived by our senses, and some few other connections between objects and between qualities of the same object. But all knowledge relating to matters of fact is particular, not general ; hence there is no science of matters of fact, no "science of bodies ;" or, to put the matter in another way, we can make certain and universal propositions only where the connection of the ideas asserted by the proposition is clearly and infallibly perceived ; but it is only in the case of such ideas as the mind forms itself in abstraction from existences that such certain and universal connection can be perceived ; with matters of fact, on the other hand, we have no certain knowledge going beyond existences, and we can make only particular propositions ; and, since there can be scientific knowledge only where we can make universal propositions, there is no science of nature.

The reason for this limited extent of our knowledge relating to matters of fact is the empirical origin and conditions of human knowledge. Since simple ideas are the ultimate elements and beginning of our knowledge, and we are absolutely dependent upon experience in having these ideas, knowledge itself is dependent very largely upon experience for its validity and extent. Take, for example, our knowledge of substance. What knowledge do we actually possess, either of material substance, or immaterial or thinking substance? The true account of our idea of material substance appears to be this : the mind takes notice that a certain number of those simple ideas it has by sensation go constantly together, "and, not imagining how these simple ideas can subsist of themselves, we accustom ourselves to suppose some substratum wherein they do subsist, and from which they result ;" but now of this substratum what idea have we but the confused idea of a something, we know not what support of qualities? and though to that complex of ideas, or to those co-existing qualities of which we have ideas, we do and must add this supposition of a substratum or support, our actual knowledge reaches no farther than the qualities themselves, and the relations we have learned by experience as existing between them.

Again, what is our knowledge of cause, or of the connection of things as cause and effect? I know with intuitive certainty that whatever comes to be must have a cause. I may know from internal experience that a cause is power or efficiency, but beyond the particular connections of cause and effect which I have observed and now perceive, what knowledge of causation do I possess that is certain and universal? And of objects themselves, is not our certain knowledge limited to experience? Since I do not know on what those qualities which make my idea of a thing—say a piece of gold—depend, and since the existence of those qualities now does not necessarily follow from their existence in the past, nor does it make necessary their continued existence; and further, since the qualities whose co-existence constitute the piece of gold as known, have, so far as I can perceive, no necessary connection with each other, nor do I know that other qualities may not co-exist with them, my actual knowledge of the particular substance is narrowly limited: all that I *certainly* know is, that this particular group of qualities has existed at such times in the past as I or others can remember, and exists now while I or others are having perceptions of it.

Once more, let me instance our idea of God. Of the existence of such a being I am certain; it is demonstrable that God exists from the fact that I exist. But what is our possible knowledge of God, unaided by revelation? What do we know of the nature and mode of existence of such a being? "If we examine the idea we have of this incomprehensible Supreme Being, we shall find that the complex idea we have of God is made of simple ideas we receive from reflection; namely, having from what we experience in ourselves got the ideas of existence and duration, of knowledge and power, of pleasure and happiness, and of several other qualities and powers, when we would frame an idea the most suitable we can to the Supreme Being, we enlarge every one of these with our idea of infinity, and so make our complex idea of God."

If we have succeeded in exhibiting in its essential features Locke's theory of knowledge, we are in a position to form a judgment respecting the influence Locke has exerted upon subsequent philosophy, and to determine the direction in which Locke's philosophy legitimately leads. It is obvious that this theory of knowledge holds in solution elements not readily adjusted, if they are indeed not radically opposed.

The only question is, whether Locke's explanation of human knowledge, if made consistent, does not issue in the philosophical skepticism of Hume, and perhaps, as consistently, in the sensualistic doctrine of Condillac and his followers. The prevailing judgment is, no doubt, that Hume is the true successor of Locke,—Berkeley's immaterialism forming a transition stage.

We cannot share this view of Locke's position in the development of modern philosophy. We by no means wish to deny Locke's profound influence upon the philosophers who trace their lineage to him; but we do not think the only consistent interpretation of Locke's teaching leads to the philosophy of Hume or to that of the French materialistic school. Hume's reduction of mind to the series of fleeting states and their fading copies as ideas, with a denial of all knowledge of the existence of a self, and of an external world, and of an Absolute Being, is no legitimate outcome of Locke's empiricism; such a nihilism is reached only by ignoring or distorting the psychological basis of Locke's system. Locke at the outset clearly presupposes and recognizes the reality of mind as something which is not the product of experience. Of the existence of the self as a thinking being, we have, according to Locke, intuitive and necessary knowledge. Locke could well assent to Des Cartes' "cogito, ergo sum." And likewise, in respect to the reality of an external world or a not-self, despite his naïve and indefensible realism, Locke remains true to the psychological fact that we do not and cannot rest satisfied with our merely suggestive states—the sense data; but we postulate a reality that is independent of our ideas, and to which our ideas must correspond if they are to be anything more than fictions of the imagination. Locke teaches that the existence of an external world is inseparable from the ideas we have of it, and therein he is true to a fundamental deliverance of consciousness.

It is this basis of psychological fact that Hume does not accept in its integrity, but takes merely the conscious state or feeling without its implicate of a subject and a something not the psychical state as the object. Now Locke, notwithstanding his limitation of knowledge respecting the self and external objects, teaches plainly that both subject and object are implicated as real existences in the simplest act of knowledge. It cannot, we think, be opposed to this interpretation of Locke, that he reduces the work of mind to the passive reception of impressions and the mere uniting of ideas to form knowledge. Such an interpretation of Locke's doctrine of ideas is possible only by converting Locke's metaphors into facts. What Locke teaches in this direction is the fact that the individual mind is absolutely dependent upon sense experience for its earliest ideas as the beginning and elements of knowledge. If in this part of the Essay Locke represents the mind as passive and receptive only, such language should be taken in connection with the abundant and explicit statements elsewhere, that the mind exercises powers peculiar to itself and is in all actual knowledge original and creative.

Should it be urged that such functions of mind are not possible if Locke's empirical explanation of knowledge is to be taken in earnest and carried to its consistent issue, it may with more justice to him be replied, we are bound to make Locke's empiricism consistent with his explicit recognition of essentially *a priori* or non-empirical factors in knowledge; and, if so, Locke's theory of knowledge may lead us in quite a different direction from that taken by Hume. We suggest that the direction in which we may seek a more consequent issue of Locke's philosophy, when interpreted from its aim and prevailing spirit, is the critical philosophy of Kant.

The problem of Kant's philosophy was really anticipated by Locke. Kant's more special problem, to determine the possibility, the conditions, and the extent of knowledge that is independent of experience, becomes, in Kant's solution of it, the more general problem of Locke, viz., to determine the certainty and the extent of human knowledge. And however widely Kant's method departs from the method of Locke, and however profound the differences are that separate in some respects the critical idealism of Kant from the naïve and hardly consistent realism of Locke, the two philosophers reach conclusions so much in agreement respecting the empirical conditions and limits of human knowledge, as to justify the assertion that it is toward Kant and critical philosophy, rather than toward Hume and his successors, that Locke's theory of knowledge legitimately tends.

BIBLIOGRAPHY.

We present the bibliography relating to Locke's life and his writings in the following scheme:

A.—LOCKE'S WRITINGS.

I. Philosophical Writings.

1. "An Epitome of the Essay Concerning Human Understanding," prepared at the request of Le Clerc, in the autumn of 1687, and published in the "Bibliothèque Universelle" for June, 1688. The original manuscript of this "Epitome" is still in existence. A number of copies of the "Epitome" were printed separately for friends of Locke, but only one of these is extant.

2. "The Essay Concerning Human Understanding. Locke's manuscript of the first edition was sent to the press in May, 1689, and the work was issued from the press probably in March of the following year. Three subsequent editions were published during the lifetime of Locke; the second edition, containing a number of changes, was issued in 1694; the third edition in 1695, and the fourth in the autumn of 1699. This last edition contained two additional chapters: the chapter upon Enthusiasm and the one upon Association of Ideas; and besides these additions the chapter upon Power had been rewritten. A French version of the Essay was executed by Pierre Costa, a friend of Le Clerc and of Locke, and published at Amsterdam in 1700, with the title, "Essai Philosophique concernant l'Entendement, où l'ón montre quelle est l'Entendue de nos Connaissances certaines et la Manière dont nous y parvenons." In 1701 a Latin version of the Essay, which had been begun by Bur-

bridge in 1695, was published in London under the title, "De Intellectu Humano."

Subsequent editions of the Essay appeared in 1723, 1729, 1742, 1750, 1755, 1758, 1774. Up to the present time upwards of forty editions of the Essay have been published, besides numerous translations in French, German, and Dutch.

3. "Essay on the Conduct of the Understanding." A writing intended by Locke to form a chapter in the fourth edition of the Essay, but left by him incomplete, and published probably by his cousin, Peter King, in 1706.

4. "Letters in Reply to Stillingfleet, the Bishop of Worcester." There were three of these letters, and they were a vindication of Locke's doctrine of knowledge against the criticisms that the Bishop of Worcester had directed against the Essay; these letters were published between the years 1692 and 1699, and two of them have been incorporated in some editions of the Essay.

II. Ethical and Theological Writings.

1. Small essay in Latin, written in 1661.
2. An unpublished essay on Toleration, 1666.
3. "Epistola de Tolerantia;" written in Holland, 1685, addressed to Locke's friend Limborch, and published at London in 1689.
4. Three writings, under the same English title, were published in 1690, 1692, and 1706; the last is only a fragment.
5. "The Reasonableness of Christianity as delivered in the Scriptures," published in 1695. Two vindications of this treatise were published in the years 1695 and 1697.
6. "A discourse on Miracles," 1706.
7. "Paraphrases and Notes on the Epistles of St. Paul to the Galatians, First and Second Corinthians, Romans, and Ephesians," 1705-7.

✓III. Political Writings.

1. Two Treatises on Government, 1690.
2. "The Fundamental Constitutions of Carolina," 1720.
3. "Some Considerations on the Economy of Lowering

the Rate of Interest and Raising the Value of Money," 1691.

4. "For Encouraging the Coining of Silver Money," 1695.

3. "Further Considerations Concerning Raising the Value of Money," 1695.

IV. *Miscellaneous Writings.*

1. "Some Thoughts Concerning Education," 1693.
2. "Memoirs Relating to the Life of Anthony, first Earl of Shaftesbury," 1720.
3. "Some Thoughts Concerning Reading," 1720.

V. *Correspondence.*

1. "Some Familiar Letters between Mr. Locke and Several of his Friends; Containing Forty-three Letters from Locke to Limborch."
2. "Letters from Locke;" in Remonstrants' Library, Amsterdam, nearly all written in Latin.
3. "Original Letters of Locke, Algernon Sidney, and Anthony, Earl of Shaftesbury." A second edition of these Letters was published in 1847, but they are not known to be extant.
4. "Letters from Relations and Friends." Containing letters of Locke to Estha Masham. Letters now in possession of Miss Palmer.
5. "Letters to Lord King."
6. "Collection Letters." In possession of Mr. Sanford Nynehead.
7. "Correspondence." In possession of Lord Lovelace.

B.—ON THE LIFE AND WRITINGS OF LOCKE.

I. Biographical.

1. Earliest account of Locke's life, "Eloge de Monsieur Locke." Published by his friend, Jean Le Clerc, in the Bibliothèque Choisie, in 1705. This Eloge was little more than a translation of two letters that had been sent to Le Clerc, one written by the third Earl of Shaftesbury,

the other by Lady Masham. A version of the Eloge was published in London in 1706. This brief account of Locke's life was re-written by Bishop Low, with some additions, for the edition of "Locke's Works," edited and published by him in 1777.

2. "The Life of John Locke, with Extracts from His Correspondence, Journals, and Commonplace Books," by Lord King, in 1830. This work contains hardly any biographical matter not contained in Le Clerc's Eloge.

3. "The Life of John Locke," by Fox Bourne, in two volumes. New York: Harper & Brothers, 1876. This work is the first attempt at a full and systematic biography of Locke.

4. "Locke," by Thomas Fowler. English Men of Letters Series. New York: Macmillan & Co., 1883; an admirable account of Locke's life and his principal writings.

5. "Locke," by Alexander Campbell Fraser, Blackwood's Philosophical Classics. Philadelphia: J. B. Lippincott Company, 1890. Article by the same author in "Encyclopædia Britannica," vol. XIV.

II. Locke's Collected Writings.

There is as yet no adequate edition of Locke's works. The edition published by Bishop Low in 1771 is still the best.

Upon the Essay the following references are given:

T. H. Green's "Philosophical Works," Vol. I. "Introduction to Hume's Philosophical Works," by the same author. The two volumes already referred to upon "Locke," the one by Thomas Fowler, and the other by Campbell Fraser. A chapter in Cousin's "Histoire de la Philosophie, au XVIII. siècle, École sensualiste, système de Locke." Webb's "Intellectualism of Locke." Leibnitz's "Nouveaux Essais sur l'Entendement Humain." Sections relating to Locke in the following Histories of Philosophy: Ueberweg, "Geschichte der Philosophie;" Erdmann, "Geschichte der Philosophie;" Falconberg, "Geschichte der Neuen Philosophie;" Kuno Fischer, "Bacon und seine Nachfolger."

THE PHILOSOPHY OF LOCKE AS CONTAINED IN THE "ESSAY CONCERNING HUMAN UNDERSTANDING."

THE PHILOSOPHY OF LOCKE.

EPISTLE TO THE READER AND INTRODUCTION.

Occasion, Purpose, and Plan of the Essay.

WERE it fit to trouble thee with the history of this Essay, I should tell thee, that five or six friends, meeting at my chamber, and discoursing on a subject very remote from this, found themselves quickly at a stand by the difficulties that rose on every side. After we had awhile puzzled ourselves, without coming any nearer a resolution of those doubts which perplexed us, it came into my thoughts, that we took a wrong course; and that, before we set ourselves upon inquiries of that nature, it was necessary to examine our own abilities, and see what objects our understandings were or were not fitted to deal with. This I proposed to the company, who all readily assented; and thereupon it was agreed, that this should be our first inquiry. Some hasty and undigested thoughts, on a subject I had never before considered, which I set down against our next meeting, gave the first entrance into this discourse, which, having been thus begun by chance, was continued by entreaty; written by incoherent parcels; and, after long intervals of neglect, resumed again, as my humor or occasions permitted; and at last, in a retirement, where an attendance on my health gave me leisure, it was brought into that order thou now seest it.

This was that which gave the first rise to this Essay concerning the Understanding. For I thought that the first step towards satisfying several inquiries the mind of man was very apt to run into, was, to take a survey of our own understandings, examine our own powers, and see to what things they were adapted.

2. *Design.*—This, therefore, being my purpose, to inquire into the original, certainty, and extent of human knowledge, together with the grounds and degrees of belief, opinion and assent, I shall not at present meddle with the physical consideration of the mind, or trouble myself to examine wherein its essence consists, or by what motions of our spirits, or alterations of our bodies, we come to have any sensation by our organs, or any ideas in our understandings; and whether those ideas do, in their formation, any or all of them, depend on matter or no; these are speculations which, however curious and entertaining, I shall decline, as lying out of my way in the design I am now upon. It shall suffice to my present purpose, to consider the discerning faculties of a man as they are employed about the objects which they have to do. In order whereunto, I shall pursue this following method :—

First, I shall inquire into the original of those ideas, notions, or whatever else you please to call them, which a man observes, and is conscious to himself he has in his mind, and the ways whereby the understanding comes to be furnished with them.

Secondly, I shall endeavor to show what knowledge

the understanding hath by those ideas, and the certainty, evidence, and extent of it.

Thirdly, I shall make some inquiry into the nature and grounds of faith or opinion ; whereby I mean, that assent which we give to any proposition as true, of whose truth yet we have no certain knowledge : and here we shall have occasion to examine the reasons and degrees of assent.

THE ORIGIN OF IDEAS AS THE ELEMENTS OR MATERIALS OF OUR KNOWLEDGE.

Before I proceed on to what I have thought on this subject, I must here, in the entrance, beg pardon of my reader for the frequent use of the word "idea" which he will find in the following treatise. It being that term which, I think, serves best to stand for whatsoever is the object of the understanding when a man thinks, I have used it to express whatever is meant by phantasm, notion, species, or whatever it is which the mind can be employed about in thinking; and I could not avoid frequently using it.

I presume it will be easily granted me, that there are such *ideas* in men's minds. Every one is conscious of them in himself; and men's words and actions will satisfy him that they are in others.

Our first inquiry, then, shall be, how they come into the mind.

Our Ideas not Innate.

It is an established opinion among some men, that there are in the understanding certain innate principles; some primary notions, κοιναὶ ἔννοιαι, characters, as it were, stamped upon the mind of man, which the soul receives in its very first being, and brings into the world with it. It would be sufficient to convince unprejudiced readers of the falseness of this supposition, if I should only show (as I hope I shall in the following parts of this discourse) how men, barely by the use of their natural faculties, may attain to all the knowledge they have, without the help of any innate impressions, and may arrive at certainty without any such original notions or principles. There is nothing more commonly taken for granted, than that there are certain principles, both speculative and practical (for they speak of both), universally agreed upon by all mankind; which therefore, they argue, must needs be constant impressions which the souls of men receive in their first beings, and which they bring into the world with them, as necessarily and really as they do any of their inherent faculties.

This argument, drawn from universal consent, has this misfortune in it, that if it were true in matter of fact, that there were certain truths wherein all mankind agreed, it would not prove them innate, if there can be any other way shown, how men may come to that universal agreement in the things they do consent in; which I presume may be done.

But yet I take liberty to say, that these propositions are so far from having an universal assent, that there are a great part of mankind to whom they are not so much as known.

No proposition can be said to be in the mind which it never yet knew, which it was never yet conscious of. For if any one may, then, by the same reason, all propositions that are true, and the mind is capable ever of assenting to, may be said to be in the mind, and to be imprinted.

To avoid this, it is usually answered, that all men know and assent to them, when they come to the use of reason ; I answer, *If reason discovered them, that would not prove them innate.*

But how can men think the use of reason necessary to discover principles that are supposed to be innate, when reason (if we may believe them) is nothing else but the faculty of deducing unknown truths from principles or propositions that are already known? That certainly can never be thought innate which we have need of reason to discover, unless, as I have said, we will have all the certain truths that reason ever teaches us to be innate. There is this farther argument in it against these ideas being innate that these characters, if they were native and original impressions, should appear fairest and clearest in those persons in whom yet we find no footsteps of them ; and it is, in my opinion, a strong presumption that they are not innate, since they are least known to those in whom, if they were innate, they must needs exert themselves with most force and vigor. For children, idiots, savages, and illiterate people, being of all others the least corrupted by custom or borrowed opinions ; learning and education having not cast their native thoughts into new moulds, nor by superinducing foreign and studied doctrines confounded those fair characters nature had written there ; one might reasonably imagine, that in their minds these innate notions should be open fairly to every one's view, as it is certain the thoughts of children do.

THE SOURCE OF OUR IDEAS.

Let us then suppose the mind to be, as we say, white paper, void of all characters, without any ideas; how comes it to be furnished? Whence comes it by that vast store, which the busy and boundless fancy of man has painted on it with an almost endless variety? Whence has it all the materials of reason and knowledge? To this I answer, in one word, From experience: in that all our knowledge is founded, and from that it ultimately derives itself. Our observation, employed either about external sensible objects, or about the internal operations of our minds, perceived and reflected on by ourselves, is that which supplies our understandings with all the materials of thinking. These two are the fountains of knowledge, from whence all the ideas we have, or can naturally have, do spring.

First. Our senses, conversant about particular sensible objects, do convey into the mind several distinct perceptions of things, according to those various ways wherein those objects do affect them; and thus we come by those ideas we have of yellow, white, heat, cold, soft, hard, bitter, sweet, and all those which we call sensible qualities; which when I say the senses convey into the mind, I mean, they from external objects convey into the mind what produces there those perceptions. This great source of most of the ideas we have, depending wholly upon our senses, and derived by them to the understanding, I call "sensation."

Secondly. The other fountain, from which experience furnisheth the understanding with ideas, is the perception of the operations of our own minds within us, as it is employed about the ideas it has got; which operations, when the soul comes to reflect on and consider, do furnish the understanding with another set of ideas which could not be had from things without; and such are perception, thinking, doubting, believing, reasoning, knowing, willing, and all the different actings of our own minds which we, being conscious of, and observing in others, do from these receive into our understandings as distinct ideas, as we do from bodies affecting our senses. This source of ideas every man has wholly in himself; and though it be not sense as having nothing to do with external objects, yet it is very like it, and might properly enough be called "internal sense." But as I call the other "sensation," so I call this "reflection," the ideas it affords being such only as the mind gets by reflecting on its own operations within itself. By reflection, then, in the following part of this discourse, I would be understood to mean that notice which the mind takes of its own operations, and the manner of them, by reason whereof there come to be ideas of these operations in the understanding. These two, I say, viz., external material things as the objects of sensation, and the operations of our own minds within as the objects of reflection, are, to me, the only originals from whence all our ideas take their beginnings. The term "operations" here, I use in a large sense, as comprehending not barely the actions of the mind about its ideas, but some sort of passions arising sometimes from them, such as is the satisfaction or uneasiness arising from any thought.

I see no reason therefore to believe that the soul thinks before the senses have furnished it with ideas to think on; and as those are increased and retained, so it comes by exercise to improve its faculty of thinking in the several parts of it; as well as afterwards, by compounding those ideas and reflecting on its own operations, it increases its stock, as well as facility in remembering, imagining, reasoning, and other modes of thinking.

Thus the first capacity of human intellect is, that the mind is fitted to receive the impressions made on it, either through the senses by outward objects, or by its own operations when it reflects on them. This is the first step a man makes towards the discovery of any thing, and the ground-work whereon to build all those notions which ever he shall have naturally in this world.

All those sublime thoughts which tower above the clouds and reach as high as heaven itself, take their rise and footing here: in all that great extent wherein the mind wanders in those remote speculations it may seem to be elevated with, it stirs not one jot beyond those ideas which sense or reflection have offered for its contemplation.

In this part the understanding is merely passive; and whether or no it will have these beginnings and, as it were, materials of knowledge, is not in its own power. For the objects of our senses do many of them obtrude their particular ideas upon our minds whether we will or no, and the operations of our minds will not let us be without at least some obscure notions of them. When the understanding is once stored with these simple ideas, it has the power to repeat, compare, and unite them, even to an almost infinite variety, and so can make at pleasure new complex ideas. But it is not in the power of the most exalted wit or enlarged understanding, by any quickness or variety of thoughts, to invent or frame one new simple idea in the mind, not taken in by the ways before mentioned; nor can any force of the understanding destroy those that are there.

CLASSIFICATION OF IDEAS.

The better to understand the nature, manner, and extent of our knowledge, one thing is carefully to be observed concerning the ideas we have; and that is, that some of them are simple, and some complex.

Though the qualities that affect our senses are, in the things themselves, so united and blended that there is no separation, no distance between them; yet it is plain the ideas they produce in the mind enter by the senses simple and unmixed. For though the sight and touch often take in from the same object at the same time different ideas—as a man sees at once motion and color, the hand feels softness and warmth in the same piece of wax—yet the simple ideas thus united in the same subject are as perfectly distinct as those that come in by different senses; the coldness and hardness which a man feels in a piece of ice being as distinct ideas in the mind as the smell and whiteness of a lily, or as the taste of sugar and smell of a rose: and there is nothing can be plainer to a man than the clear and distinct perception he has of those simple ideas; which, being each in itself uncompounded, contains in it nothing but one uniform appearance or conception in the mind, and is not distinguishable into different ideas.

As simple ideas are observed to exist in several combinations united together, so the mind has a power to consider several of them united together as one idea; and that not only as they are united in external object, but as itself has joined them. Ideas thus made up of several simple ones put together I call "complex;" such as are beauty, gratitude, a man, an army, the universe; which, though complicated of various simple ideas or complex ideas made up of simple ones, yet are, when the mind pleases, considered each by itself as one entire thing, and signified by one name.

The better to conceive the ideas we receive from sensation, it may not be amiss for us to consider them in reference to the different ways whereby they make their approaches to our minds, and make themselves perceivable by us.

First, then, there are some which come into our minds by one sense only.

Secondly. There are others that convey themselves into the mind by more senses than one.

Thirdly. Others that are had from reflection only.

Fourthly. There are some that make themselves way, and are suggested to the mind, by all the ways of sensation and reflection.

SOME OF OUR SIMPLE IDEAS CONSIDERED.

1. *Idea of Solidity.*

I think it will be needless to enumerate all the particular simple ideas belonging to each sense. Nor indeed is it possible if we would, there being a great many more of them belonging to most of the senses than we have names for.

I shall therefore, in the account of simple ideas I am here giving, content myself to set down only such as are most material to our present purpose, or are in themselves less apt to be taken notice of, though they are very frequently the ingredients of our complex ideas; amongst which I think I may well account "solidity," which therefore I shall treat of in the next chapter.

There is no idea which we receive more constantly from sensation than solidity. Whether we move or rest, in what posture soever we are, we always feel something under us that supports us, and hinders our farther sinking downwards; and the bodies which we daily handle make us perceive that whilst they remain between them, they do, by an insurmountable force, hinder the approach of the parts of our hands that press them.

This, of all others, seems the idea most intimately connected with and essential to body, so as nowhere else to be found or imagined but only in matter.

This is the idea belongs to body, whereby we conceive it to fill space. The idea of which filling of space is, that where we imagine any space taken up by a solid substance, we conceive it so to possess it that it excludes all other solid substances, and will for ever hinder any two other bodies, that move towards one another in a straight line, from coming to touch one another, unless it removes from between them in a line not parallel to that which they move in. This idea of it, the bodies which we ordinary handle sufficiently furnish us with.

This resistance, whereby it keeps other bodies out of the space which it possesses, is so great that no force, how great soever, can surmount it. All the bodies in the world, pressing a drop of water on all sides, will never be able to overcome the resistance which it will make, as soft as it is, to their approaching one another, till it be removed out of their way: whereby our idea of solidity is distinguished both from pure space, which is capable neither of resistance nor motion, and from the ordinary idea of hardness.

Solidity is hereby also differenced from hardness, in that solidity consists in repletion, and so an utter exclusion of other bodies out of the space it possesses; but hardness in a firm cohesion of the parts of matter, making up masses of a sensible bulk, so that the whole does not easily change its figure.

2. *Ideas of Perception and Willing.*

The idea of perception, and idea of willing, we have from reflection.—The two great and principal actions of the mind, which are most frequently considered, and which are so frequent that every one that pleases may take notice of them in himself, are these two:

perception or thinking, and volition or willing. The power of thinking is called "the understanding," and the power of volition is called "the will;" and these two powers or abilities in the mind are denominated "faculties." Of some of the modes of these simple ideas of reflection, such as are remembrance, discerning, reasoning, judging, knowledge, faith, etc., I shall have occasion to speak hereafter.

3. *Ideas of Pleasure and Pain.*

There be other simple ideas which convey themselves into the mind by all the ways of sensation and reflection ; viz., pleasure or delight, and its opposite, pain or uneasiness ; power, existence, unity.

Delight or uneasiness, one or other of them, join themselves to almost all our ideas both of sensation and reflection ; and there is scarce any affection of our senses from without, any retired thought of our mind within, which is not able to produce in us pleasure or pain. By "pleasure" and "pain" I would be understood to signify whatsoever delights or molests us ; whether it arises from the thoughts of our minds, or any thing operating on our bodies. For whether we call it "satisfaction, delight, pleasure, happiness," etc., on the one side ; or "uneasiness, trouble, pain, torment, anguish, misery," etc., on the other ; they are still but different degrees of the same thing, and belong to the ideas of pleasure and pain, delight or uneasiness ; which are the names I shall most commonly use for those two sorts of ideas.

4. *Ideas of Existence and Unity.*

Existence and unity are two other ideas that are suggested to the understanding by every object without, and every idea within. When ideas are in our minds, we consider them as being actually there, as well as we consider things to be actually without us: which is, that they exist, or have existence: <u>and</u> whatever we can consider as one thing, whether a real being or idea, suggests to the understanding the idea of unity.

5. *Idea of Power.*

Power also is another of those simple ideas which we receive from sensation and reflection. For, observing in ourselves that we can at pleasure move several parts of our bodies which were at rest, the effects also that natural bodies are able to produce in one another occurring every moment to our senses, we both these ways get the idea of power.

6. *Idea of Succession.*

Besides these there is another idea, which though suggested by our senses, yet is more constantly offered us by what passes in our own minds; and that is the idea of succession. For if we look immediately into ourselves, and reflect on what is observable there, we shall find our ideas always, whilst we are awake or have any thought, passing in train, one going and another coming without intermission.

More Particular Examination of Some of the Simple Ideas from Sensation.

Concerning the simple ideas of sensation it is to be considered, that whatsoever is so constituted in nature as to be able by affecting our senses to cause any perception in the mind, doth thereby produce in the understanding a simple idea; which, whatever be the external cause of it, when it comes to be taken notice of by our discerning faculty, it is by the mind looked on and considered there to be a real positive idea in the understanding, as much as any other whatsoever; though perhaps the cause of it be but a privation in the subject.

Thus the ideas of heat and cold, light and darkness, white and black, motion and rest, are equally clear and positive ideas in the mind; though perhaps some of the causes which produce them are barely privations in those subjects from whence our senses derive those ideas. These the understanding, in its view of them, considers all as distinct positive ideas without taking notice of the causes that produce them; which is an inquiry not belonging to the idea as it is in the understanding, but to the nature of the thing existing without us. These are two very different things, and carefully to be distinguished; it being one thing to perceive and know the idea of white or black, and quite another to examine what kind of particles they must be, and how ranged in the superficies, to make any object appear white or black.

To discover the nature of our ideas the better, and to discourse of them intelligibly, it will be convenient to distinguish them, as they are ideas or perceptions in our minds, and as they are modifications of matter in the bodies that cause such perceptions in us; that so we may not think (as perhaps usually is done) that they are exactly the images and resemblances of something inherent in the subject; most of those of sensation being in the mind no more the likeness of something existing without us than the names that stand for them are the likeness of our ideas, which yet upon hearing they are apt to excite in us.

Thus a snowball having the power to produce in us the ideas of white, cold, and round, the powers to produce those ideas in us as they are in the snowball, I call "qualities;" and as they are sensations or perceptions in our understandings, I call them "ideas;" which ideas, if I speak of them sometimes as in the things themselves, I would be understood to mean those qualities in the objects which produce them in us.

Qualities thus considered in bodies are, First, such as are utterly inseparable from the body, in what estate soever it be; such as, in all the alterations and changes it suffers, all the force can be used upon it, it constantly keeps; and such as sense constantly finds in every particle of matter which has bulk enough to be perceived, and the mind finds inseparable from every particle of matter, though less than to make itself singly be perceived by our senses: *v. g.*, take a grain of wheat, divide it into two parts, each part has still solidity, extension, figure, and mobility; divide it again, and it retains still the same qualities: and so divide it on till the parts become insensible, they must retain still each of them all those qualities. For, division (which is all that a mill or pestle or any other body does upon another, in reducing it to insensible parts) can never take away either solidity, extension, figure, or mobility from any body, but only makes two or more distinct separate masses of matter of that which was but one before; all which distinct masses, reckoned as so many distinct bodies, after division, make a certain number. These I call *original* or *primary* qualities of body, which I think we may observe to produce simple ideas in us, viz., solidity, extension, figure, motion or rest, and number.

Secondary qualities. — Secondly. Such qualities, which in truth are nothing in the objects themselves, but powers to produce various sensations in us by their primary qualities, *i. e.*, by colors, sounds, tastes, etc., these I call *secondary* qualities. To these might be added a third sort, which are allowed to be barely powers, though they are as much real qualities in the subject as those which I, to comply with the common way of speaking, call qualities, but, for distinction, *secondary* qualities. For, the power in fire to produce a new color or consistence in wax or clay by its primary qualities, is as much a quality in fire as the power it has to produce in me a new idea or sensation of warmth or burning, which I felt not before, by the same primary qualities, viz., the bulk, texture, and motion of its insensible parts.

The next thing to be considered is how bodies produce ideas in us; and that is manifestly by impulse, the only way which we can conceive bodies operate in.

If, then, external objects be not united to our minds when they produce ideas in it, and yet we perceive these original qualities in such of them as singly fall under our senses, it is evident that some motion must be thence continued by our nerves or animal spirits, by some parts of our bodies, to the brain or the seat of sensation, there to produce in our minds the particular ideas we have of them.

After the same manner that the ideas of these original qualities are produced in us, we may conceive that the ideas of secondary qualities are also produced, viz., by the operation of insensible particles on our senses. Let us suppose at present that the different motions and figures, bulk and number, of such particles, affecting the several organs of our senses, produce in us those different sensations which we have from the colors and smells of bodies, *v. g.*, that a violet, by the impulse of such insensible particles of matter of peculiar figures and bulks, and in different degrees and modifications of their motions, causes the ideas of the blue color and sweet scent of that flower to be produced in our minds. From whence I think it is easy to draw this observation, that the ideas of primary qualities of bodies are resemblances of them, and their patterns do really exist in the bodies themselves; but the ideas produced in us by these secondary qualities have no resemblance of them at all. There is nothing like our ideas existing in the bodies themselves. They are, in the bodies we denominate from them, only a power to produce those sensations in us; and what is sweet, blue, or warm in idea, is but the certain bulk, figure, and motion of the insensible parts in the bodies themselves, which we call so.

The particular bulk, number, figure, and motion of the parts of fire or snow are really in them, whether any one's senses perceive them or no; and therefore they may be called *real* qualities, because they really exist in those bodies. But light, heat, whiteness, or coldness, are no more really in them than sickness or pain is in manna. Take away the sensation of them;

let not the eyes see light or colors, nor the ears hear sounds; let the palate not taste, nor the nose smell; and all colors, tastes, odors, and sounds, as they are such particular ideas, vanish and cease, and are reduced to their <u>causes, *i. e.*, bulk, figure</u>, and motion of parts.

Let us consider the red and white colors in porphyry: hinder light but from striking on it, and its colors vanish; it no longer produces any such ideas in us. Upon the return of light, it produces these appearances on us again.

The qualities then that are in bodies, rightly considered, are of three sorts:

First. The bulk, figure, number, situation, and motion or rest of their solid parts; those are in them whether <u>we perceive them or no</u>; and when they are of that size that we can discover them, we have by these an idea of the thing as it is in itself, as is plain in artificial things. These I call *primary* qualities.

Secondly. The power that is in any body, by reason of its insensible primary qualities, to operate after a peculiar manner on any of our senses, and thereby produce in us the different ideas of several colors, sounds, smells, tastes, etc. These are usually called *<u>sensible</u>* qualities.

Thirdly. The power that is in any body, by reason of the particular constitution of its primary qualities, to make such a change in the bulk, figure, texture, and motion of another body, as to make it operate on our senses differently from what it did before. Thus the sun has a power to make wax white, and fire, to make lead fluid. These are usually called "powers."

SOME FUNCTIONS OF MIND INVOLVED IN HAVING SIMPLE IDEAS.

I. Perception.

What perception is, every one will know better by reflecting on what he does himself, when he sees, hears, feels, etc., or thinks, than by any discourse of mine. Whoever reflects on what passes in his own mind, cannot miss it ; and if he does not reflect, all the words in the world cannot make him have any notion of it.

This is certain, that whatever alterations are made in the body, if they reach not the mind ; whatever impressions are made on the outward parts, if they are not taken notice of within ; there is no perception. Fire may burn our bodies with no other effect than it does a billet, unless the motion be continued to the brain, and there the sense of heat or idea of pain be produced in the mind.

We are farther to consider concerning perception, that the ideas we receive by sensation are often in grown people altered by the judgment without our taking notice of it. When we set before our eyes a round globe of any uniform color, *v. g.*, gold, alabaster, or jet, it is certain that the idea thereby imprinted in our mind is of a flat circle variously shadowed, with several degrees of light and brightness coming to our eyes. But we having by use been accustomed to perceive what kind of appearance convex bodies are wont to make in us, what alterations are made in the reflections of light by the difference of the sensible figures of bodies, the judgment presently, by an habitual custom, alters the appearances into their causes : so that, from that which truly is variety of shadow or color collecting the figure, it makes it pass for a mark of figure, and frames to itself the perception of a convex figure and an uniform color; when the idea we receive from thence is only a plane variously colored, as is evident in painting.

This, in many cases, by a settled habit in things whereof we have frequent experience, is performed so constantly and so quick, that we take that for the perception of our sensation which is an idea formed by our judgment; so that one, viz., that of sensation, serves only to excite the other, and is scarce taken notice of itself; as a man who reads or hears with attention and understanding, takes little notice of the characters or sounds, but of the ideas that are excited in him by them.

Nor need we wonder that this is done with so little notice, if we consider how very quick the actions of the mind are performed: for as itself is thought to take up no space, to have no extension, so its actions seem to require no time, but many of them seem to be crowded into an instant. I speak this in comparison to the actions of the body. Any one may easily observe this in his own thoughts who will take the pains to reflect on them.

Perception, then, being the first step and degree towards knowledge, and the inlet of all the materials of it, the fewer senses any man as well as any other creature hath, and the fewer and duller the impressions are that are made by them, and the duller the faculties are that are employed about them, the more remote are they from that knowledge which is to be found in some men. But this, being in great variety of degrees (as may be perceived amongst men), cannot certainly be discovered in the several species of animals, much less in their particular individuals.

2. *Retention and Memory.*

The next faculty of the mind, whereby it makes a farther progress towards knowledge, is that which I call retention or the keeping of those simple ideas which from sensation or reflection it hath received. This is done two ways. First, by keeping the idea which is brought into it for some time actually in view, which is called contemplation.

The other way of retention is the power to revive again in our minds those ideas which after imprinting have disappeared, or have been as it were laid aside out of sight ; and thus we do, when we conceive heat or light, yellow or sweet, the object being removed. This is memory, which is, as it were, the storehouse of our ideas. For the narrow mind of man, not being capable of having many ideas under view and consideration at once, it was necessary to have a repository to lay up those ideas, which at another time it might have use of. But our ideas being nothing but actual perceptions in the mind, which cease to be anything when there is no perception of them, this laying up of our ideas in the repository of the memory signifies no more but this,—that the mind has a power, in many cases, to revive perceptions which it has once had, with this additional perception annexed to them,—that it has had them before. And in this sense it is that our ideas are said to be in our memories, when indeed they are actually nowhere, but only there is an ability in the mind when it will to revive them again, and, as it were, paint them anew on itself, though some with more, some with less, difficulty; some more lively, and others more obscurely. Attention and repetition help much to the fixing any ideas in the memory; but those which naturally at first make the deepest and most lasting impression, are those which are accompanied with pleasure or pain.

Ideas fade in the memory.—Concerning the several degrees of lasting wherewith ideas are imprinted on the memory, we may observe, that some of them have been produced in the understanding by an object affecting the senses once only, and no more than once; others, that have more than once offered themselves to the senses, have yet been little taken notice of; the mind either heedless as in children, or otherwise employed as in men, intent only on one thing, not setting the stamp deep into itself; and in some, where they are set to with care and repeated impressions, either through the temper of the body or some other default, the memory is very weak.

This farther is to be observed concerning ideas lodged in the memory, and upon occasion revived by the mind,—that they are not only (as the word "revive" imports) none of them new ones, but also that the mind takes notice of them as of a former impression, and renews its acquaintance with them as with ideas it had known before. So that though ideas formerly imprinted are not all constantly in view, yet in remembrance they are constantly known to be such as have been formerly imprinted, *i. e.*, in view, and taken notice of before by the understanding.

3. *Discerning.*

Another faculty we may take notice of in our minds, is that of discerning and distinguishing between the several ideas it has. It is not enough to have a confused perception of something in general : unless the mind had a distinct perception of different objects and their qualities, it would be capable of very little knowledge ; though the bodies that affect us were as busy about us as they are now, and the mind were continually employed in thinking. On this faculty of distinguishing one thing from another, depends the evidence and certainty of several even very general propositions, which have passed for innate truths ; because men, overlooking the true cause why those propositions find universal assent, impute it wholly to native uniform impressions : whereas it in truth depends upon this clear discerning faculty of the mind, whereby it perceives two ideas to be the same or different.

4. *Comparing.*

The comparing them one with another, in respect of extent, degrees, time, place, or any other circumstances, is another operation of the mind about its ideas, and is that upon which depends all that large tribe of ideas comprehended under relation; which of how vast an extent it is, I shall have occasion to consider hereafter.

How far brutes partake in this faculty is not easy to determine; I imagine they have it not in any great degree: for though they probably have several ideas distinct enough, yet it seems to me to be the prerogative of human understanding, when it has sufficiently distinguished any ideas so as to perceive them to be perfectly different, and so consequently two, to cast about and consider in what circumstances they are capable to be compared. And therefore, I think, beasts compare not their ideas farther than some sensible circumstances annexed to the objects themselves.

5. *Compounding*.

The next operation we may observe in the mind about its ideas is composition; whereby it puts together several of those simple ones it has received from sensation and reflection, and combines them into complex ones. Under this of composition may be reckoned also that of enlarging; wherein though the composition does not so much appear as in more complex ones, yet it is nevertheless as putting several ideas together, though of the same kind. Thus, by adding several units together we make the idea of a dozen, and putting together the repeated ideas of several perches we frame that of a furlong.

Conclusion.

And thus I have given a short and, I think, true history of the first beginnings of human knowledge, whence the mind has its first object, and by what steps it makes its progress to the laying in and storing up those ideas out of which is to be framed all the knowledge it is capable of; wherein I must appeal to experience and observation whether I am in the right.

These are my guesses concerning the means whereby the understanding comes to have and retain simple ideas and the modes of them, with some other operations about them. I proceed now to examine some of these simple ideas and their modes a little more particularly.

✓ COMPLEX IDEAS—GENERAL ACCOUNT.

We have hitherto considered those ideas, in the reception whereof the mind is only passive, which are those simple ones received from sensation and reflection before mentioned, whereof the mind cannot make one to itself, nor have any idea which does not wholly consist of them. But as the mind is wholly passive in the reception of all its simple ideas, so it exerts several acts of its own, whereby out of its simple ideas, as the materials and foundations of the rest, the other are framed. The acts of the mind wherein it exerts its power over its simple ideas are chiefly these three: (1.) Combining several simple ideas into one compound one; and thus all complex ideas are made. (2.) The second is bringing two ideas, whether simple or complex, together, and setting them by one another, so as to take a view of them at once, without uniting them into one; by which it gets all its ideas of relations. (3.) The third is separating them from all other ideas that accompany them in their real existence; this is called "abstraction:" and thus all its general ideas are made. This shows man's power and its way of operation to be muchwhat the same in the material and intellectual world. For, the materials in both being such as he has no power over, either to make or destroy, all that man can do is either to unite them together, or to set them by one another, or wholly separate them. I shall here begin with the first of these in the consideration of complex ideas, and come to the other two in their due places.

Complex ideas, however compounded and decompounded, though their number be infinite, and the variety endless wherewith they fill and entertain the thoughts of men, yet I think they may be all reduced under these three heads: 1. Modes. 2. Substances. 3. Relations.

First. "Modes" I call such complex ideas which, however compounded, contain not in them the supposition of subsisting by themselves, but are considered as dependences on or affections of substances; such are the ideas signified by the words, "triangle, gratitude, murder," etc.

Of these modes there are two sorts which deserve distinct consideration. First. There are some which are only variations or different combinations of the same simple idea, without the mixture of any other, as a dozen, or score; which are nothing but the ideas of so many distinct units added together: and these I call "simple modes," as being contained within the bounds of one simple idea. Secondly. There are others compounded of simple ideas, of several kinds, put together to make one complex one; *v. g.*, beauty, consisting of a certain composition of color and figure, causing delight in the beholder; theft, which, being the concealed change of the possession of any thing, without the consent of the proprietor, contains, as is visible, a combination of several ideas of several kinds: and these I call "mixed modes."

Secondly. The ideas of substances are such combinations of simple ideas as are taken to represent distinct particular things subsisting by themselves, in which the supposed or confused idea of substance, such as it is, is always the first and chief. Thus, if to substance be joined the simple idea of a certain dull, whitish color with certain degrees of weight, hardness, ductility, and fusibility, we have the idea of lead; and the combination of the ideas of a certain sort of figure, with the powers of motion, thought, and reasoning, joined to substance, make the ordinary idea of a man. Now of substances also there are two sorts of ideas, one of single substances, as they exist separately, as of a man or a sheep; the other of several of those put together, as an army of men or flock of sheep; which collective ideas of several substances thus put together, are as much each of them one single idea as that of a man or an unit.

Thirdly. The last sort of complex ideas is that we call "Relation," which consists in the consideration and comparing one idea with another. Of these several kinds we shall treat in their order.

A MORE PARTICULAR ACCOUNT OF SOME OF OUR COMPLEX IDEAS.

I. *The Idea of Space.*

I shall begin with the simple idea of space. I have showed above (chap. iv.), that we get the idea of space both by our sight and touch: which I think is so evident that it would be as needless to go to prove that men perceive by their sight a distance between bodies of different colors, or between the parts of the same body, as that they see colors themselves; nor is it less obvious that they can do so in the dark by feeling and touch.

This space considered barely in length between any two beings, without considering any thing else between them, is called "distance;" if considered in length, breadth, and thickness, I think it may be called "capacity;" the term "extension" is usually applied to it, in what manner soever considered.

Each different distance is a different modification of space, and each idea of any different distance or space is a simple mode of this idea.

There is another modification of this idea, which is nothing but the relation which the parts of the termination of extension or circumscribed space have amongst themselves. This the touch discovers in sensible bodies, whose extremities come within our reach; and the eye takes both from bodies and colors, whose boundaries are within its view : where, observing how the extremities terminate either in straight lines which meet at discernible angles, or in crooked lines wherein no angles can be perceived, by considering these as they relate to one another in all parts of the extremities of any body or space, it has that idea we call " figure."

Another idea coming under this head and belonging to this tribe, is that we call " place." As in simple space we consider the relation of distance between any two bodies or points, so in our idea of place we consider the relation of distance betwixt any thing and any two or more points, which are considered as keeping the same distance one with another, and so considered as at rest ; for when we find any thing at the same distance now which it was yesterday from any two or more points, which have not since changed their distance one with another, and with which we then compared it, we say it hath kept the same place ; but if it hath sensibly altered its distance with either of those points, we say it hath changed its place ; though, vulgarly speaking in the common notion of place, we do not always exactly observe the distance from precise points, but from large portions of sensible objects to which we consider the thing place to bear relation, and its distance from which we have some reason to observe.

There are some that would persuade us that body and extension are the same thing ; who either change the signification of words, which I would not suspect them of, they having so severely condemned the philosophy of others because it hath been too much placed in the uncertain meaning or deceitful obscurity of doubtful or insignificant terms. If therefore they mean by body and extension, the same that other people do, viz., by body, something that is solid and extended, whose parts are separable and movable different ways; and by extension only the space that lies between the extremities of these solid coherent parts, and which is possessed by them, they confound very different ideas one with another. For I appeal to every man's own thoughts, whether the idea of space be not as distinct from that of solidity, as it is from the idea of scarlet color? It is true, solidity cannot exist without extension, neither can scarlet color exist without extension; but this hinders not but that they are distinct ideas. Many ideas require others as necessary to their existence or conception, which yet are very distinct ideas.

Body, then, and extension, it is evident, are two distinct ideas. For,

First. Extension includes no solidity nor resistance to the motion of body, as body does.

Secondly. The parts of pure space are inseparable one from the other; so that the continuity cannot be separated, neither really nor mentally. For I demand of any one to remove any part of it from another with which it is continued, even so much as in thought.

Thirdly. The parts of pure space are immovable, which follows from their inseparability; motion being nothing but change of distance between any two things: but this cannot be between parts that are inseparable; which therefore must needs be at perpetual rest one amongst another.

But the question being here, whether the idea of space or extension be the same with the idea of body, it is not necessary to prove the real existence of a *vacuum*, but the idea of it; which it is plain men have when they inquire and dispute whether there be a *vacuum* or no. For if they had not the idea of space without body, they could not make a question about its existence; and if their idea of body did not include in it something more than the bare idea of space, they could have no doubt about the plenitude of the world; and it would be as absurd to demand whether there were space without body, as whether there were space without space, or body without body, since these were but different names of the same idea.

2. *The Idea of Duration.*

To understand time and eternity aright, we ought with attention to consider what idea it is we have of duration, and how we came by it. It is evident to any one who will but observe what passes in his own mind, that there is a train of ideas which constantly succeed one another in his understanding as long as he is awake. Reflection on these appearances of several ideas one after another in our minds, is that which furnishes us with the idea of succession; and the distance between any parts of that succession, or between the appearance of any two ideas in our minds, is that we call duration. For whilst we are thinking, or whilst we receive successively several ideas in our minds, we know that we do exist; and so we call the existence or the continuation of the existence of ourselves or any thing else commensurate to the succession of any ideas in our minds, the duration of ourselves, or any such other thing co-existing with our thinking.

That we have our notions of succession and duration from this original, viz., from reflection on the train of ideas which we find to appear one after another in our own minds, seems plain to me, in that we have no perception of duration but by considering the train of ideas that take their turns in our understandings. When that succession of ideas ceases, our perception of duration ceases with it; which every one clearly experiments in himself whilst he sleeps soundly, whether an hour, or a day, or a month, or a year; of which duration of things whilst he sleeps or thinks not he has no perception at all, but it is quite lost to him; and the moment wherein he leaves off to think till the moment he begins to think again, seems to him to have no distance, by which it is to me very clear that men derive their ideas of duration from their reflection on the train of the ideas they observe to succeed one another in their own understandings; without which observation they can have no notion of duration, whatever may happen in the world.

Thus, by reflecting on the appearance of various ideas one after another in our understandings, we get the notion of succession; which if any one should think we did rather get from our observation of motion by our senses, he will perhaps be of my mind, when he considers that even motion produces in his mind an idea of succession no otherwise than as it produces there a continued train of distinguishable ideas, and we have as clear an idea of succession and duration by the train of other ideas succeeding one another in our minds without the idea of any motion, as by the train of ideas caused by the uninterrupted sensible change of distance between two bodies which we have from motion; and therefore we should as well have the idea of duration, were there no sense of motion at all.

But the distinction of days and years having depended on the motion of the sun, it has brought this mistake with it,—that it has been thought that motion and duration were the measure one of another.

Time is duration set out by measures.—Having thus got the idea of duration, the next thing natural for the mind to do is, to get some measure of this common duration, whereby it might judge of its different lengths, and consider the distinct order wherein several things exist; without which a great part of our knowledge would be confused, and a great part of history be rendered very useless. This consideration of duration, as set out by certain periods, and marked by certain measures or epochs, is that, I think, which most properly we call "time."

Nothing then could serve well for a convenient measure of time but what has divided the whole length of its duration into apparently equal portions by constantly repeated periods. What portions of duration are not distinguished or considered as distinguished and measured by such periods come not so properly under the notion of time, as appears by such phrases as these, viz., "before all time," and "when time shall be no more." Whereas any constant periodical appearance or alteration of ideas in seemingly equidistant spaces of duration, if constant and universally observable, would have as well distinguished the intervals of time as those that have been made use of.

We must therefore carefully distinguish betwixt duration itself and the measures we make use of to judge of its length. Duration in itself is to be considered as going on in one constant, equal, uniform course. But none of the measures of it which we make use of can be known to do so: nor can we be assured that their assigned parts or periods are equal in duration one to another; for two successive lengths of duration, however measured, can never be demonstrated to be equal. All that we can do for a measure of time, is to take such as have continual successive appearances at seemingly equidistant periods; of which seeming equality we have no other measure but such as the train of our own ideas have lodged in our memories, with the concurrence of other probable reasons, to persuade us of their equality.

By the same means, therefore, and from the same original, that we come to have the idea of time, we have also that idea which we call "eternity," viz., having got the idea of succession and duration, by reflecting on the train of our own ideas, caused in us either by the natural appearances of those ideas coming constantly of themselves into our waking thoughts, or else caused by external objects successively affecting our senses; and having from the revolutions of the sun got the ideas of certain lengths of duration, we can in our thoughts add such lengths of duration to one another as often as we please, and apply them, so added, to durations past or to come: and this we can continue to do on, without bounds or limits, and proceed *in infinitum*, and apply thus the length of the annual motion of the sun to duration, supposed before the sun's or any other motion had its being.

And thus I think it is plain, that from those two fountains of all knowledge before mentioned, viz., reflection and sensation, we get the ideas of duration, and the measures of it.

For, First, by observing what passes in our minds, how our ideas there in train constantly some vanish, and others begin to appear, we come by the idea of succession.

Secondly. By observing a distance in the parts of this succession, we get the idea of duration.

Thirdly. By sensation observing certain appearances, at certain regular and seeming equidistant periods, we get the ideas of certain lengths or measures of duration, as minutes, hours, days, years, etc.

Fourthly. By being able to repeat those measures of time, or ideas of stated length of duration in our minds, as often as we will, we can come to imagine duration where nothing does really endure or exist; and thus we imagine to-morrow, next year, or seven years hence.

Fifthly. By being able to repeat any such idea of any length of time, as of a minute, a year, or an age, as often as we will in our own thoughts, and add them one to another, without ever coming to the end of such addition, any nearer than we can to the end of number, to which we can always add, we come by the idea of eternity, as the future eternal duration of our souls, as well as the eternity of that infinite Being which must necessarily have always existed.

Sixthly. By considering any part of infinite duration, as set out by periodical measures, we come by the idea of what we call "time" in general.

Time in general is to duration as place to expansion. They are so much of those boundless oceans of eternity and immensity, as is set out and distinguished from the rest as it were by land-marks; and so are made use of to denote the position of finite real beings, in respect one to another, in those uniform infinite oceans of duration and space.

There is one thing more wherein space and duration have a great conformity; and that is, though they are justly reckoned amongst our simple ideas, yet none of the distinct ideas we have of either is without all manner of composition; it is the very nature of both of them to consist of parts: but their parts being all of the same kind, and without the mixture of any other idea, hinder them not from having a place amongst simple ideas. Could the mind, as in number, come to so small a part of extension or duration as excluded divisibility, that would be, as it were, the indivisible unit or idea; by repetition of which, it would make its more enlarged ideas of extension and duration. But since the mind is not able to frame an idea of any space without parts, instead thereof it makes use of the common measures, which by familiar use in each country have imprinted themselves on the memory.

Expansion and duration have this farther agreement, that though they are both considered by us as having parts, yet their parts are not separable one from another, no, not even in thought; though the parts of bodies from whence we take our measure of the one, and the parts of motion, or rather the succession of ideas in our minds, from whence we take the measure of the other, may be interrupted and separated, as the one is often by rest, and the other is by sleep, which we call rest too.

But yet there is this manifest difference between them, that the ideas of length which we have of expansion are turned every way, and so make figure, and breadth, and thickness; but duration is but as it were the length of one straight line extended *in infinitum*, not capable of multiplicity, variation, or figure, but is one common measure of all existence whatsoever, wherein all things, whilst they exist, equally partake.

To conclude: expansion and duration do mutually embrace and comprehend each other; every part of space being in every part of duration, and every part of duration in every part of expansion. Such a combination of two distinct ideas is, I suppose, scarce to be found in all that great variety we do or can conceive, and may afford matter to farther speculation.

3. *The Idea of Number.*

Amongst all the ideas we have, as there is none suggested to the mind by more ways, so there is none more simple, than that of unity, or one.

By repeating this idea in our minds, and adding the repetitions together, we come by the complex ideas of the modes of it. Thus by adding one to one we have the complex idea of a couple: by putting twelve units together we have the complex idea of a dozen; and a score, or a million, or any other number.

This is not so in other simple modes, in which it is not so easy, nor perhaps possible, for us to distinguish betwixt two approaching ideas, which yet are really different. For who will undertake to find a difference between the white of this paper and that of the next degree to it? or can form distinct ideas of even the least excess in extension?

The clearness and distinctness of each mode of number from all others, even those that approach nearest, makes me apt to think that demonstrations in numbers, if they are not more evident and exact than in extension, yet they are more general in their use, and more determinate in their application. Because the ideas of numbers are more precise and distinguishable than in extension, where every equality and excess are not so easy to be observed or measured.

4. *The Idea of Infinity.*

He that would know what kind of idea it is to which we give the name of "infinity," cannot do it better than by considering to what infinity is by the mind more immediately attributed, and then how the mind comes to frame it.

Finite and infinite seem to me to be looked upon by the mind as the modes of quantity, and to be attributed primarily in their first designation only to those things which have parts, and are capable of increase or diminution by the addition or subtraction of any the least part; and such are the ideas of space, duration, and number, which we have considered in the foregoing chapters. But yet when we apply to that first and supreme Being our idea of infinite, in our weak and narrow thoughts, we do it primarily in respect of his duration and ubiquity; and, I think, more figuratively to his power, wisdom, and goodness, and other attributes, which are properly inexhaustible and incomprehensible, etc. For when we call them infinite, we have no other idea of this infinity but what carries with it some reflection on and intimation of that number or extent of the acts or objects of God's power, wisdom, and goodness, which can never be supposed so great or so many, which these attributes will not always surmount and exceed, let us multiply them in our thoughts as far as we can, with all the infinity of endless number.

As for the idea of finite, there is no great difficulty. The obvious portions of extension that affect our senses carry with them into the mind the idea of finite. The difficulty is, how we come by those boundless ideas of eternity and immensity, since the objects which we converse with come so much short of any approach or proportion to that largeness.

Every one that has any idea of any stated lengths of space, as a foot, finds that he can repeat that idea; and, joining it to the former, make the idea of two feet, and, by the addition of a third, three feet, and so on, without ever coming to an end of his additions, whether of the same idea of a foot, or, if he pleases, of doubling it, or any other idea he has of any length, as a mile, or diameter of the earth, or of the *orbis magnus;* for whichsoever of these he takes, and how often soever he doubles or any otherwise multiplies it, he finds that, after he has continued this doubling in his thoughts and enlarged his idea as much as he pleases, he has no more reason to stop, nor is one jot nearer the end of such addition than he was at first setting out : the power of enlarging his idea of space by farther additions remaining still the same, he hence takes the idea of infinite space.

I think it is not an insignificant subtilty if I say that we are carefully to distinguish between the idea of *the infinity of space* and the idea of *a space infinite ;* the first is nothing but a supposed endless progression of the mind over what repeated ideas of space it pleases ; but to have actually in the mind the idea of a space infinite, is to suppose the mind already passed over, and actually to have a view of all those repeated ideas of space which an endless repetition can never totally represent to it : which carries in it a plain contradiction ; for of any space, duration, or number, let them be never so great, they are still finite ; but when we suppose an inexhaustible remainder, from which we remove all bounds, and wherein we allow the mind an endless progression of thought, without ever completing the idea, there we have our idea of infinity ; which though it seems to be pretty clear when we consider nothing else in it but the negation of an end, yet when we would frame in our minds the idea of an infinite space or duration, that idea is very obscure and confused, because it is made up of two parts very different, if not inconsistent.

Though it be hard, I think, to find any one so absurd as to say he has the positive idea of an actual infinite number, yet there be those who imagine they have positive ideas of infinite duration and space. It would, I think, be enough to destroy any such positive idea of infinite to ask him that has it, whether he could add to it or no? which would easily show the mistake of such a positive idea. We can, I think, have no positive idea of any space or duration which is not made up of, and commensurate to, repeated numbers of feet or yards, or days and years; which are the common measures whereof we have the idea in our minds, and whereby we judge of the greatness of these sort of quantities. And therefore, since an idea of infinite space or duration must needs be made up of infinite parts, it can have no other infinity than that of number, capable still of farther addition; but not an actual positive idea of a number infinite.

The idea of infinite has, I confess, something of positive in all those things we apply it to. When we would think of infinite space or duration, we at first step usually make some very large idea, as, perhaps, of millions of ages or miles, which possibly we double and multiply several times. All that we thus amass together in our thoughts is positive, and the assemblage of a great number of positive ideas of space or duration. But what still remains beyond this, we have no more a positive, distinct notion of, than a mariner has of the depth of the sea, where, having let down a large portion of his sounding-line, he reaches no bottom: whereby he knows the depth to be so many fathoms, and more; but how much that *more* is, he hath no distinct notion at all: and could he always supply new line, and find the plummet always sink without ever stopping, he would be something in the posture of the mind reaching after a complete and positive idea of infinity.

SOME OTHER SIMPLE MODES CONSIDERED.

1. *Modes of Thinking.*

When the mind turns its view inwards upon itself, and contemplates its own actions, thinking is the first that occurs. In it the mind observes a great variety of modifications, and from thence receives distinct ideas. Thus the perception which actually accompanies and is annexed to any impression on the body made by an external object, being distinct from all other modifications of thinking, furnishes the mind with a distinct idea which we call "sensation;" which is, as it were, the actual entrance of any idea into the understanding by the senses. The same idea, when it again recurs without the operation of the like object on the external sensory, is "remembrance:" if it be sought after by the mind, and with pain and endeavor found, and brought again in view, it is "recollection:" if it be held there long under attentive consideration, it is "contemplation": when ideas float in our mind without any reflection or regard of the understanding, it is that which the French call *rêverie;* our language has scarce a name for it: when the ideas that offer themselves (for, as I have observed in another place, whilst we are awake there will always be a train of ideas succeeding one another in our minds) are taken notice of, and, at it were, registered in the memory, it is "attention."

These are some few instances of those various modes of thinking which the mind may observe in itself, and so have as distinct ideas of as it hath of white and red, a square or a circle. I do not pretend to enumerate them all, nor to treat at large of this set of ideas which are got from reflection; that would be to make a volume. It suffices to my present purpose to have shown here, by some few examples, of what sort these ideas are, and how the mind comes by them; especially since I shall have occasion hereafter to treat more at large of reasoning, judging, volition, and knowledge, which are some of the most considerable operations of the mind, and modes of thinking.

2. *The Idea of Power.*

The mind being every day informed, by the senses, of the alteration of those simple ideas it observes in things without, and taking notice how one comes to an end and ceases to be, and another begins to exist which was not before; reflecting also, on what passes within itself, and observing a constant change of its ideas, sometimes by the impression of outward objects on the senses, and sometimes by the determination of its own choice; and concluding from what it has so constantly observed to have been, that the like changes will for the future be made in the same things by like agents, and by the like ways; considers in one thing the possibility of having any of its simple ideas changed, and in another the possibility of making that change; and so comes by that idea which we call "power."

Power thus considered is twofold ; viz., as able to make, or able to receive, any change : the one may be called "active," and the other "passive," power.

I confess power includes in it some kind of relation,—a relation to action or change ; as, indeed, which of our ideas, of what kind soever, when attentively considered, does not? For our ideas of extension, duration, and number, do they not all contain in them a secret relation of the parts? Figure and motion have something relative in them much more visibly. And sensible qualities, as colors and smells, etc., what are they but the powers of different bodies in relation to our perception, etc.?

3. *Mixed Modes.*

That the mind, in respect of its simple ideas, is wholly passive, and receives them all from the existence and operations of things, such as sensation or reflection offers them, without being able to make any one idea, experience shows us. But if we attentively consider these ideas I call "mixed modes" we are now speaking of, we shall find their original quite different. The mind often exercises an active power in making these several combinations : for, it being once furnished with simple ideas, it can put them together in several compositions, and so make variety of complex ideas, without examining whether they exist so together in nature. And hence, I think, it is that these ideas are called "notions ;" as if they had their original and constant existence more in the thoughts of men, than in the reality of things ; and to form such ideas it sufficed that the mind puts the parts of them together, and that they were consistent in the understanding, without considering whether they had any real being: though I do not deny but several of them might be taken from observation, and the existence of several simple ideas so combined as they are put together in the understanding.

THE IDEA OF SUBSTANCE.

The mind being, as I have declared, furnished with a great number of the simple ideas conveyed in by the senses, as they are found in exterior things, or by reflection on its own operations, takes notice, also, that a certain number of these simple ideas go constantly together; which being presumed to belong to one thing, and words being suited to common apprehensions, and made use of for quick dispatch, are called, so united in one subject, by one name; which, by inadvertency, we are apt afterward to talk of and consider as one simple idea, which indeed is a complication of many ideas together: because, as I have said, not imagining how these simple ideas can subsist by themselves, we accustom ourselves to suppose some _substratum_ wherein they do subsist, and from which they do result; which therefore we call "substance."

But if any one will examine himself concerning his notion of pure substance in general, he will find he has no other idea of it at all, but only a supposition of he knows not what support of such qualities which are capable of producing simple ideas in us; which qualities are commonly called "accidents." If any one should be asked, "What is the subject wherein color or weight inheres?" he would have nothing to say but, "The solid extended parts." And if he were demanded, "What is it that solidity and extension inhere in," he would not be in a much better case than the Indian before mentioned, who, saying that the world was supported by a great elephant, was asked, what the elephant rested on? to which his answer was, "A great tortoise:" but being again pressed to know what gave support to the broadbacked tortoise, replied,—something, he knew not what.

An obscure and relative idea of substance in general being thus made, we come to have the ideas of particular sorts of substances, by collecting such combinations of simple ideas as are by experience and observation of men's senses taken notice of to exist together, and are therefore supposed to flow from the particular internal constitution or unknown essence of that substance. Thus we come to have the ideas of a man, horse, gold, water, etc., of which substances, whether any one has any other clear idea, farther than of certain simple ideas co-existing together, I appeal to every one's own experience. It is the ordinary qualities observable in iron or a diamond, put together, that make the true complex idea of those substances, which a smith or a jeweller commonly knows better than a philosopher; who, whatever substantial forms he may talk of, has no other idea of those substances than what is framed by a collection of those simple ideas which are to be found in them. Only we must take notice, that our complex ideas of substances, besides all these simple ideas they are made up of, have always the confused idea of something to which they belong and in which they subsist.

Hence, when we talk or think of any particular sort of corporeal substances, as horse, stone, etc., though the idea we have of either of them be but the complication or collection of those several simple ideas of sensible qualities which we used to find united in the thing called "horse" or "stone;" yet because we cannot conceive how they should subsist alone, nor one in another, we suppose them existing in, and supported by, some common subject; which support we denote by the name "substance," though it be certain we have no clear or distinct idea of that thing we suppose a support.

The same happens concerning the operations of the mind; viz., thinking, reasoning, fearing, etc., which we concluding not to subsist of themselves, nor apprehending how they can belong to body, or be produced by it, we are apt to think these the actions of some other substance, which we call "spirit;" whereby yet it is evident, that having no other idea or notion of matter, but something wherein those many sensible qualities which affect our senses do subsist; by supposing a substance wherein thinking, knowing, doubting, and a power of moving, etc., do subsist; we have as clear a notion of the substance of spirit as we have of body: the one being supposed to be (without knowing what it is) the *substratum* to those simple ideas we have from without; and the other supposed (with a like ignorance of what it is) to be the *substratum* to those operations which we experiment in ourselves within.

For our idea of substance is equally obscure, or none at all, in both; it is but a supposed I know-not-what, to support those ideas we call "accidents." It is for want of reflection that we are apt to think that our senses show us nothing but material things.

Every act of sensation, when duly considered, gives us an equal view of both parts of nature, the corporeal and spiritual. For, whilst I know, by seeing or hearing, etc., that there is some corporeal being without me, the object of that sensation, I can more certainly know that there is some spiritual being within me that sees and hears. This I must be convinced cannot be the action of bare insensible matter, nor even could be without an immaterial thinking being.

The ideas that make our complex ones of corporeal substances are of these three sorts. First, The ideas of the primary qualities of things which are discovered by our senses, and are in them even when we perceive them not: such are the bulk, figure, number, situation, and motion of the parts of bodies, which are really in them, whether we take notice of them or no. Secondly, The sensible secondary qualities which, depending on these, are nothing but the powers those substances have to produce several ideas in us by our senses; which ideas are not in the things themselves otherwise than as anything is in its cause. Thirdly, The aptness we consider in any substance to give or receive such alterations of primary qualities as that the substance so altered should produce in us different ideas from what it did before; these are called "active and passive powers:" all which powers, as far as we have any notice or notion of them, terminate only in sensible simple ideas.

And thus we have seen what kind of ideas we have of substances of all kinds, wherein they consist, and how we come by them. From whence, I think, it is very evident:

First. That all our ideas of the several sorts of

substances are nothing but collections of simple ideas, with a supposition of something to which they belong, and in which they subsist; though of this supposed something we have no clear distinct idea at all.

Secondly. That all the simple ideas that, thus united in one common substratum, make up our complex ideas of several sorts of substances, are no other but such as we have received from sensation or reflection. So that even in those which we think are most intimately acquainted with, and come nearest the comprehension of our most enlarged conceptions, we cannot reach beyond those simple ideas. And even in those which seem most remote from all we have to do with, and do infinitely surpass anything we can perceive in ourselves by reflection, or discover by sensation in other things, we can attain to nothing but those simple ideas which we originally received from sensation or reflection ; as is evident in the complex ideas we have of angels, and particularly of God himself.

Thirdly. That most of the simple ideas that make up our complex ideas of substances, when truly considered, are only powers, however we are apt to take them for positive qualities : *v. g.*, the greatest part of the ideas that make our complex idea of gold are yellowness, great weight, ductility, fusibility, and solubility in *aqua regia*, etc., all united together in an unknown substratum ; all which ideas are nothing else but so many relations to other substances, and are not really in the gold considered barely in itself, though they depend on those real and primary qualities of its internal constitution, whereby it has a fitness differently to operate and be operated on by several other substances.

Besides these complex ideas of several single substances, as of man, horse, gold, violet, apple, etc., the mind hath also "complex collective ideas" of substances ; which I so call, because such ideas are made up of many particular substances considered together, as united into one idea, and which so joined are looked on as one ; *v. g.*, the idea of such a collection of men as make an army, though consisting of a great number of distinct substances, is as much one idea as the idea of a man : and the great collective idea of all bodies whatsoever, signified by the name " world," is as much one idea as the idea of any the least particle of matter in it ; it sufficing to the unity of any idea, that it be considered as one representation or picture, though made up of ever so many particulars.

These collective ideas of substances the mind makes by its power of composition, and uniting, severally, either simple or complex ideas into one, as it does by the same faculty make the complex ideas of particular substances, consisting of an aggregate of divers simple ideas united in one substance : and as the mind, by putting together the repeated ideas of unity, makes the collective mode or complex idea of any number, as a score, or a gross, etc., so by putting together several particular substances, it makes collective ideas of substances, as a troop, an army, a swarm, a city, a fleet : each of which every one finds that he represents to his own mind by one idea, in one view ; and so under that notion considers those several things as perfectly one, as one ship, or one atom.

The Idea of Relation.

Besides the ideas, whether simple or complex, that the mind has of things, as they are in themselves, there are others it gets from their comparison one with another. The understanding, in the consideration of any thing, is not confined to that precise object: it can carry any idea, as it were, beyond itself, or, at least, look beyond it to see how it stands in conformity to any other. When the mind so considers one thing, that it does, as it were, bring it to and set it by another, and carry its view from one to the other: this is, as the words import, "relation" and "respect;" and the denominations given to positive things, intimating that respect, and serving as marks to lead the thoughts beyond the subject itself denominated to something distinct from it, are what we call "relatives;" and the things so brought together, "related."

The Idea of Relation—How Formed.

This farther may be observed, that the ideas of relation may be the same in men who have far different ideas of the things that are related, or that are thus compared: *v. g.*, those who have far different ideas of a man, may yet agree in the notion of a father: which is a notion superinduced to the substance, or man, and refers only to an act of that thing called "man," whereby he contributed to the generation of one of his own kind, let man be what it will.

Relation and Things Related.

The nature therefore of relation consists in the referring or comparing two things one to another; from which comparison one or both comes to be denominated. And if either of those things be removed or cease to be, the relation ceases, and the denomination consequent to it, though the other receive in itself no alteration at all : *v. g.*, Caius, whom I consider to-day as a father, ceases to be so to-morrow, only by the death of his son, without any alteration made in himself. Nay, barely by the mind's changing the object, to which it compares any thing, the same thing is capable of having contrary denominations at the same time : *v. g.*, Caius, compared to several persons, may truly be said to be older and younger, stronger and weaker, etc.

1. *The Idea of Cause and Effect.*

Having laid down these premises concerning relation in general, I shall now proceed to show in some instances, how all the ideas we have of relation are made up, as the others are, only of simple ideas ; and that they all, how refined or remote from sense soever they seem, terminate at last in simple ideas. I shall begin with the most comprehensive relation, wherein all things that do or can exist are concerned ; and that is the relation of cause and effect. The idea whereof, how derived from the two fountains of all our knowledge, sensation and reflection, I shall in the next place consider.

In the notice that our senses take of the constant vicissitude of things, we cannot but observe that several particular qualities and substances begin to exist ; and that they receive this their existence from the due application and operation of some other being. From this observation we get our ideas of cause and effect. That which produces any simple or complex idea, we denote by the general name "cause;" and that which is produced, "effect." Thus finding that in that substance which we call "wax" fluidity, which is a simple idea that was not in it before, is constantly produced by the application of a certain degree of heat, we call the simple idea of heat, in relation to fluidity in wax, *the cause* of it, and fluidity *the effect*.

2. *The Ideas of Identity and Diversity.*

Another occasion the mind often takes of comparing, is, the very being of things, when, considering any thing as existing at any determined time and place, we compare it with itself existing at another time, and thereon form the ideas of identity and diversity. When we see any thing to be in any place in any instant of time, we are sure (be it what it will) that it is that very thing, and not another, which at that same time exists in another place, how like and undistinguishable soever it may be in all other respects: and in this consists identity, when the ideas it is attributed to, vary not at all from what they were that moment wherein we consider their former existence, and to which we compare the present. For we never finding, nor conceiving it possible, that two things of the same kind should exist in the same place at the same time, we rightly conclude that whatever exists any where at any time, excludes all of the same kind, and is there itself alone. When therefore we demand whether any thing be the same or no, it refers always to something that existed such a time in such a place, which it was certain at that instant was the same with itself and no other: from whence it follows, that one thing cannot have two beginnings of existence, nor two things one beginning, it being impossible for two things of the same kind to be or exist in the same instant, in the very same place, or one and the same thing in different places. For example: Could two bodies be in the same place at the same time, then those two parcels of matter must be one and the same, take them great or little; nay, all bodies must be one and the same. For by the same reason that two particles of matter may be in one place, all bodies may be in one place: which, when it can be supposed, takes away the distinction of identity and diversity, of one and more, and renders it ridiculous.

This, though it seems easier to conceive in simple substances or modes, yet, when reflected on, is not more difficult in compounded ones, if care be taken to what it is applied; *v. g.*, let us suppose an atom, *i. e.*, a continued body under one immutable superficies, existing in a determined time and place; it is evident, that, considered in any instant of its existence, it is, in that instant, the same with itself. For, being at that instant what it is and nothing else, it is the same, and so must continue as long as its existence is continued; for so long it will be the same and no other. In like manner, if two or more atoms be joined together into the same mass, every one of those atoms will be the same, by the foregoing rule: and whilst they exist united together, the mass, consisting of the same atoms, must be the same mass, or the same body, let the parts be ever so differently jumbled: but if one of these atoms be taken away, or one new one added, it is no longer the same mass, or the same body. In the state of living creatures, their identity depends not on a mass of the same particles, but on something else. For in them the variation of great parcels of matter alters not the identity; an oak, growing from a plant to a great tree, and then lopped, is still the same oak: and a colt, grown up to a horse, sometimes fat, sometimes lean, is all the while the same horse: though, in both these cases, there may be a manifest change of the parts; so that truly they are not either of them the same masses of matter, though there be truly one of them the same oak, and the other the same horse. The reason whereof is, that, in these two cases of a mass of matter and a living body, identity is not applied to the same thing.

We must therefore consider wherein an oak differs from a mass of matter; and that seems to me to be in this: That the one is only the cohesion of particles of matter any how united: the other such a disposition of them as constitutes the parts of an oak, and such an organization of those parts as is fit to receive and distribute nourishment, so as to continue and frame the wood, bark, and leaves, etc., of an oak, in which consists the vegetable life. That being then one plant which has such an organization of parts in one coherent body, partaking of one common life, it continues to be the same plant as long as it partakes of the same life, though that life be communicated to new particles of matter vitally united to the living plant in a like continued organization, comformable to that sort of plants.

This also shows wherein the identity of the same

man consists; viz., in nothing but a participation of the same continued life, by constantly fleeting particles of matter, in succession vitally united to the same organized body. He that shall place the identity of man in anything else, but, like that of other animals, in one fitly organized body, taken in any one instant, and from thence continued under one organization of life in several successively fleeting particles of matter united to it, will find it hard to make an embryo one of years, mad, and sober, the same man, by any supposition that will not make it possible for Seth, Ishmael, Socrates, Pilate, St. Austin, and Cæsar Borgia, to be the same man.

It is not therefore unity of substance that comprehends all sorts of identity, or will determine it in every case: but, to conceive and judge of it aright, we must consider what idea the word it is applied to stands for: it being one thing to be the same substance, another the same man, and a third the same person, if "person, man, and substance," are three names standing for three different ideas; for such as is the idea belonging to that name, such must be the identity: which, if it had been a little more carefully attended to, would possibly have prevented a great deal of that confusion which often occurs about this matter, with no small seeming difficulties, especially concerning personal identity, which therefore we shall in the next place a little consider.

This being premised, to fine wherein personal identity consists, we must consider what "person" stands for; which, I think, is a thinking intelligent being, that has reason and reflection, and can consider itself as itself, the same thinking thing, in different times and places; which it does only by that consciousness which is inseparable from thinking, and it seems to me essential to it: it being impossible for any one to perceive, without perceiving that he does perceive. When we see, hear, smell, taste, feel, meditate, or will any thing, we know that we do so. Thus it is always as to our present sensations and perceptions: and by this every one is to himself that which he calls "self;" it not being considered, in this case, whether the same self be continued in the same or diverse substances. For since consciousness always accompanies thinking, and it is that that makes every one to be what he calls "self," and thereby distinguishes himself from all other thinking things; in this alone consists personal identity, *i. e.*, the sameness of a rational being: and as far as this consciousness can be extended backwards to any past action or thought, so far reaches the identity of that person; it is the same self now it was then; and it is by the same self with this present one that now reflects on it, that that action was done.

But it is farther inquired, whether it be the same identical substance? This, few would think they had reason to doubt of, if these perceptions, with their consciousness, always remained present in the mind, whereby the same thinking thing would be always consciously present, and, as would be thought, evidently the same to itself. But that which seems to make the difficulty is this, that this consciousness being interrupted always by forgetfulness, there being no moment of our lives wherein we have the whole train of all our past actions before our eyes in one view; but even the best memories losing the sight of one part whilst they are viewing another; and we sometimes, and that the greatest part of our lives, not reflecting on our past selves, being intent on our present thoughts, and, in sound sleep, having no thoughts at all, or, at least, none with that consciousness which remarks our waking thoughts: I say, in all these cases, our consciousness being interrupted, and we losing the sight of our past selves, doubts are raised whether we are the same thinking thing, *i. e.*, the same substance, or no? For it being the same consciousness that makes a man be himself to himself, personal identity depends on that only, whether it be annexed only to one individual substance, or can be continued in a succession of several substances. For as far as any intelligent being can repeat the idea of any past action with the same consciousness it had of it at first, and with the same consciousness it has of any present action; so far it is the same personal self. For it is by the consciousness it has of its present thoughts and actions that it is self to itself now, and so will be the same self, as far as the same consciousness can extend to actions past or to come; and would be by distance of time, or change of substance, no more two persons than a man be two men, by wearing other clothes to-day than he did yesterday, with a long or short sleep between: the same consciousness uniting those distant actions into the same person, whatever substances contributed to their production.

But the question is, Whether, if the same substance

which thinks be changed, it can be the same person, or remaining the same, it can be different persons?

And to this I answer, First, This can be no question at all to those who place thought in a purely material, animal constitution, void of an immaterial substance. For, whether their supposition be true or no, it is plain they conceive personal identity preserved in something else than identity of substance; as animal identity is preserved in identity of life, and not of substance. And therefore those who place thinking in an immaterial substance only, before they can come to deal with these men, must show why personal identity cannot be preserved in the change of immaterial substances, or variety of particular immaterial substances, as well as animal identity is preserved in the change of material substances, or variety of particular bodies: unless they will say, it is one immaterial spirit that makes the same life in brutes, as it is one immaterial spirit that makes the same person in men, which the Cartesians at least will not admit, for fear of making brutes thinking things too.

But next, as to the first part of the question, Whether, if the same thinking substance (supposing immaterial substances only to think) be changed, it can be the same person? I answer, That cannot be resolved but by those who know what kind of substances they are that do think, and whether the consciousness of past actions can be transferred from one thinking substance to another. I grant, were the same consciousness the same individual action, it could not; but it being but a present representation of a past action, why it may not be possible that *that* may be represented to the mind to have been *which* really never was, will remain to be shown. But that which we call "the same consciousness" not being the same individual act, why one intellectual substance may not have represented to it as done by itself what it never did, and was perhaps done by some other agent; why, I say, such a representation may not possibly be without reality of matter of fact, as well as several representations in dreams are, which yet, whilst dreaming, we take for true, will be difficult to conclude from the nature of things. But yet, to return to the question before us, it must be allowed, that if the same consciousness (which, as has been shown, is quite a different thing from the same numerical figure or motion in body) can be transferred from one thinking substance to another, it will be possible that two thinking substances may make but one person. For the same consciousness being preserved, whether in the same or different substances, the personal identity is preserved.

Self is that conscious thinking thing (whatever substance made up of, whether spiritual or material, simple or compounded, it matters not) which is sensible or conscious of pleasure and pain, capable of happiness or misery, and so is concerned for itself, as far as that consciousness extends. That with which the consciousness of this present thinking thing can join itself makes the same person, and is one self with it, and with nothing else; and so attributes to itself and owns all the actions of that thing as its own, as far as that consciousness reaches, and no farther; as every one who reflects will perceive.

SOME FURTHER OBSERVATIONS UPON OUR IDEAS.

1. *Clear and Obscure Ideas.*

Our simple ideas are clear, when they are such as the objects themselves, from whence they were taken, did or might, in a well-ordered sensation or perception, present them. Whilst the memory retains them thus, and can produce them to the mind whenever it has occasion to consider them, they are clear ideas. So far as they either want any thing of that original exactness, or have lost any of their first freshness, and are, as it were, faded or tarnished by time, so far are they obscure. Complex ideas, as they are made up of simple ones, so they are clear when the ideas that go to their composition are clear: and the number and order of those simple ideas, that are the ingredients of any complex one, is determinate and certain.

The cause of obscurity in simple ideas seems to be either dull organs or very slight and transient impressions made by the objects, or else a weakness in the memory, not able to retain them as received. If the organs or faculties of perception, like wax over-hardened with cold, will not receive the impression of the seal, from the usual impulse wont to imprint it; or, like wax of a temper too soft, will not hold it well when well imprinted; or else supposing the wax of a temper fit, but the seal not applied with a sufficient force to make a clear impression : in any of these cases, the print left by the seal will be obscure.

2. *Real and Fantastical Ideas.*

Besides what we have already mentioned concerning ideas, other considerations belong to them, in reference to things from whence they are taken, or which they may be supposed to represent ; and thus, I think, they may come under a threefold distinction.

First, Our simple ideas are all real, all agree to the reality of things ; not that they are all of them the images or representations of what does exist ; but being in us the effects of powers in things without us, ordained by our Maker to produce in us such sensations, they are real ideas in us whereby we distinguish the qualities that are really in things themselves.

Secondly, Mixed modes and relations having no other reality but what they have in the minds of men, there is nothing more required to those kinds of ideas to make them real but that they be so framed that there be a possibility of existing conformable to them. These ideas, being themselves archetypes, cannot differ from their archetypes, and so cannot be chimerical, unless any one will jumble together in them inconsistent ideas. Indeed, as any of them have the names of a known language assigned to them, by which he that has them in his mind would signify them to others, so bare possibility of existing is not enough ; they must have a conformity to the ordinary signification of the name that is given them, that they may not be thought fantastical : as if a man would give the name of "justice" to that idea which common use calls "liberality." But this fantasticalness relates more to propriety of speech, than reality of ideas. For a man to be undisturbed in danger, sedately to consider what is fittest to be done, and to execute it steadily, is a mixed mode or a complex idea of an action which may exist. But to be undisturbed in danger, without using one's reason or industry, is what is also possible to be; and so is as real an idea as the other. Though the first of these, having the name "courage" given to it, may, in respect of that name, be a right or wrong idea: but the other, whilst it has not a common received name of any known language assigned to it, is not capable of any deformity, being made with no reference to anything but itself.

Thirdly, Our complex ideas of substances, being made all of them in reference to things existing without us, and intended to be representations of substances as they really are, are no farther real than as they are such combinations of simple ideas as are really united, and co-exist in things without us.

3. *Adequate and Inadequate Ideas.*

Of our real ideas, some are adequate, and some are inadequate. Those I call "adequate" which perfectly represent those archetypes which the mind supposes them taken from; which it intends them to stand for, and to which it refers them. Inadequate ideas are such which are but a partial or incomplete representation of those archetypes to which they are referred. Upon which account it is plain,

First, That all our simple ideas are adequate. Because being nothing but the effects of certain powers in things, fitted and ordained by God to produce such sensations in us, they cannot but be correspondent and adequate to those powers: and we are sure they agree to the reality of things.

Secondly, Our complex ideas of modes, being voluntary collections of simple ideas which the mind puts together, without reference to any real archetypes or standing patterns existing any where, are and cannot but be adequate ideas.

Therefore these complex ideas of modes, when they are referred by the mind, and intended to correspond, to the ideas in the mind of some other intelligent being, expressed by the names we apply to them, they may be very deficient, wrong, and inadequate; because they agree not to that which the mind designs to be their archetype and pattern; in which respect only an idea of modes can be wrong, imperfect, or inadequate. And on this account, our ideas of mixed modes are the most liable to be faulty of any other; but this refers more to proper speaking, than knowing right.

Thirdly, What ideas we have of substances, I have above showed. Now, those ideas have in the mind a double reference: (1.) Sometimes they are referred to a supposed real essence of each species of things. (2.) Sometimes they are only designed to be pictures and representations in the mind of things that do exist by ideas of those qualities that are discoverable in them. In both which ways, these copies of those originals and archetypes are imperfect and inadequate.

For since the powers or qualities that are observable by us are not the real essence of that substance, but depend on it, and flow from it, any collection whatsoever of these qualities cannot be the real essence of that thing. Whereby it is plain that our ideas of substances are not adequate; are not what the mind intends them to be. Besides, a man has no idea of substance in general, nor knows what substance is in itself.

THE ASSOCIATION OF IDEAS.

Some of our ideas have a natural correspondence and connection one with another; it is the office and excellency of our reason to trace these, and hold them together in that union and correspondence which is founded in their peculiar beings. Besides these, there is another connection of ideas wholly owing to chance or custom: ideas that in themselves are not at all of kin, come to be so united in some men's minds that it is very hard to separate them; they always keep in company, and the one no sooner at any time comes into the understanding but its associate appears with it; and if they are more than two which are thus united, the whole gang, always inseparable, show themselves together.

This strong combination of ideas, not allied by nature, the mind makes in itself either voluntarily or by chance; and hence it comes in different men to be very different, according to their different inclinations, educations, interests, etc. Custom settles habits of thinking in the understanding, as well as of determining in the will, and of motions in the body; all which seem to be but trains of motion in the animal spirits, which, once set a-going, continue in the same steps they have been used to, which, by often treading, are worn into a smooth path, and the motion in it becomes easy, and as it were natural. As far as we can comprehend thinking, thus ideas seem to be produced in our minds; or if they are not, this may serve to explain their following one another in an habitual train, when once they are put into that track, as well as it does to explain such motions of the body.

This wrong connection in our minds of ideas, in themselves loose and independent one of another, has such an influence, and is of so great force, to set us awry in our actions, as well moral as natural, passions, reasonings, and notions themselves, that perhaps there is not any one thing that deserves more to be looked after.

A man receives a sensible injury from another, thinks on the man and that action over and over, and, by ruminating on them strongly or much in his mind, so cements those two ideas together, that he makes them almost one; never thinks on the man, but the pain and displeasure he suffered comes into his mind with it, so that he scarce distinguishes them, but has as much an aversion for the one as the other. Thus hatreds are often begotten from slight and almost innocent occasions, and quarrels propagated and continued in the world.

Ideas in our minds, when they are there, will operate according to their natures and circumstances: and here we see the cause why time cures certain affections, which reason, though in the right and allowed to be so, has not power over, nor is able against them to prevail with those who are apt to hearken to it in other cases.

UPON WORDS.

Having thus given an account of the original sorts and extent of our ideas, with several other considerations about these (I know not whether I may say) instruments, or materials, of our knowledge; the method I at first proposed to myself, would now require that I should immediately proceed to show what use the understanding makes of them, and what knowledge we have by them. This was that which, in the first general view I had of this subject, was all that I thought I should have to do: but upon a nearer approach, I find that there is so close a connection between ideas and words, and our abstract ideas and general words have so constant a relation one to another, that it is impossible to speak clearly and distinctly of our knowledge, which all consists in propositions, without considering first the nature, use, and signification of language; which therefore must be the business of the next book.

1. *The Use of Language.*

Man, though he have great variety of thoughts, and such from which others as well as himself might receive profit and delight, yet they are all within his own breast, invisible, and hidden from others, nor can of themselves be made appear. The comfort and advantage of society not being to be had without communication of thoughts, it was necessary that man should find out some external sensible signs, whereby those invisible ideas which his thoughts are made up of might be made known to others. For this purpose nothing was so fit, either for plenty or quickness, as those articulate sounds which, with so much ease and variety, he found himself able to make. Thus we may conceive how words, which were by nature so well adapted to that purpose, come to be made use of by men as the signs of their ideas; not by any natural connection that there is between particular articulate sounds and certain ideas, for then there would be but one language amongst all men; but by a voluntary imposition, whereby such a word is made arbitrarily the mark of such an idea. The use, then, of words is to be sensible marks of ideas, and the ideas they stand for are their proper and immediate signification.

The use men have of these marks being either to record their own thoughts for the assistance of their own memory, or, as it were, to bring out their ideas, and lay them before the view of others: words in their primary or immediate signification stand for nothing but the ideas in the mind of him that uses them, how imperfectly soever or carelessly those ideas are collected from the things which they are supposed to represent. When a man speaks to another, it is that he may be understood; and the end of speech is, that those sounds, as marks, may make known his ideas to the hearer. That, then, which words are the marks of are the ideas of the speaker: nor can any one apply them, as marks, immediately to any thing else but the ideas that he himself hath.

2. *The Signification of Names.*

Though all words, as I have shown, signify nothing immediately but the ideas in the mind of the speaker, yet, upon a nearer survey, we shall find that the names of simple ideas, mixed modes (under which I comprise relations too), and natural substances, have each of them something peculiar, and different from the other.

First, The names of simple ideas and substances, with the abstract ideas in the mind which they immediately signify, intimate also some real existence, from which was derived their original pattern. But the names of mixed modes terminate in the idea that is in the mind, and lead not the thoughts any further, as we shall see more at large in the following chapter.

Secondly, The names of simple ideas and modes signify always the real as well as nominal essence of their species. But the names of natural substances signify rarely, if ever, any thing but barely the nominal essences of those species, as we shall show in the chapter that treats of the names of substances in particular.

Thirdly, The names of simple ideas are not capable of any definitions; the names of all complex ideas are. It has not, that I know, hitherto been taken notice of by any body, what words are, and what are not, capable of being defined : the want whereof is (as I am apt to think) not seldom the occasion of great wrangling and obscurity of men's discourses, whilst some demand definitions of terms that cannot be defined ; and others think they ought to rest satisfied in an explication made by a more general word and its restriction (or, to speak in terms of art, by a genus and difference), when even after such definition made according to rule, those who hear it have often no more a clear conception of the meaning of the word than they had before.

This being premised, I say, that "the names of simple ideas," and those only, "are incapable of being defined." The reason whereof is this, that the several terms of a definition signifying several ideas, they can all together by no means represent an idea which has no composition at all: and therefore a definition (which is properly nothing but the showing the meaning of one word by several others, not signifying each the same thing) can in the names of simple ideas have no place.

And therefore he that has not before received into his mind, by the proper inlet, the simple idea which any word stands for, can never come to know the signification of that word by any other words or sounds whatsoever, put together according to any rules of definition. The only way is by applying to his senses the proper object; and so producing that idea in him for which he has learned the name already. But though the names of simple ideas have not the help or definition to determine their signification, yet that hinders not but that they are generally less doubtful and uncertain than those of mixed modes and substances; because they standing only for one simple perception, men, for the most part, easily and perfectly agree in their signification, and there is little room for mistake and wrangling about their meaning. There is neither a multiplicity of simple ideas to be put together, which makes the doubtfulness in the names of mixed modes ; nor a supposed, but an unknown, real essence, with properties depending thereon, the precise number whereof are also unknown, which makes the difficulty in the names of substances. But, on the contrary, in simple ideas the whole signification of the name is known at once, and consists not of parts, whereof more or less being put in, the idea may be varied, and so the signification of its name be obscure or uncertain.

The names of simple ideas, substances, and mixed modes have also this difference, that those of mixed modes stand for ideas perfectly arbitrary : those of substances are not perfectly so, but refer to a pattern, though with some latitude : and those of simple ideas are perfectly taken from the existence of things, and are not arbitrary at all.

All things that exist being particulars, it may perhaps be thought reasonable that words, which ought to be conformed to things, should be so too, I mean in their signification : but yet we find the quite contrary. The far greatest part of words, that make all languages, are general terms : which has not been the effect of neglect or chance, but of reason and necessity.

First, It is impossible that every particular thing should have a distinct peculiar name. For the signification and use of words depending on that connection which the mind makes between its ideas and the sounds it uses as signs of them, it is necessary, in the application of names to things, that the mind should have distinct ideas of the things, and retain also the particular name that belongs to every one, with its peculiar appropriation to that idea. But it is beyond the power of human capacity to frame and retain distinct ideas of all the particular things we meet with: every bird and beast men saw, every tree and plant that affected the senses, could not find a place in the most capacious understanding. If it be looked on as an instance of a prodigious memory, that some generals have been able to call every soldier in their army by his proper name, we may easily find a reason why men have never attempted to give names to each sheep in their flock, or crow that flies over their heads; much less to call every leaf of plants or grain of sand that came in their way by a peculiar name.

Secondly, If it were possible, it would yet be useless, because it would not serve to the chief end of language. Men would in vain heap up names of particular things, that would not serve them to communicate their thoughts.

Thirdly, But yet granting this also feasible (which I think is not), yet a distinct name for every particular thing would not be of any great use for the improvement of knowledge: which, though founded in particular things, enlarges itself by general views: to which things reduced into sorts under general names, are properly subservient.

The next thing to be considered is, how general words come to be made. For, since all things that exist are only particulars, how come we by general terms, or where find we those general natures they are supposed to stand for? Words become general by being made the signs of general ideas: and ideas become general by separating from them the circumstances of time, and place, and any other ideas that may determine them to this or that particular existence. By this way of abstraction they are made capable of representing more individuals than one; each of which, having in it a conformity to that abstract idea, is (as we call it) of that sort.

But, to deduce this a little more distinctly, it will not perhaps be amiss to trace our notions and names from their beginning, and observe by what degrees we proceed, and by what steps we enlarge our ideas from our first infancy. There is nothing more evident than that the ideas of the persons children converse with (to instance in them alone), are, like the persons themselves, only particular. The ideas of the nurse and the mother are well framed in their minds; and, like pictures of them there, represent only those individuals. The names they first gave to them are confined to these individuals; and the names of " nurse" and "mamma" the child uses, determine themselves to those persons. Afterwards, when time and a larger acquaintance has made them observe that there are a great many other things in the world, that, in some common agreements of shape and several other qualities, resemble their father and mother, and those persons they have been used to, they frame an idea which they find those many particulars do partake in; and to that they give, with others, the name "man," for example. And thus they come to have a general name, and a general idea. Wherein they make nothing new, but only leave out of the complex idea they had of Peter and James, Mary and Jane, that which is peculiar to each, and retain only what is common to them all.

For, let any one reflect, and then tell me wherein

does his idea of "man" differ from that of "Peter" and "Paul," or his idea of "horse" from that of "Bucephalus," but in the leaving out something that is peculiar to each individual, and retaining so much of those particular complex ideas of several particular existences as they are found to agree in ? Of the complex ideas signified by the names "man" and "horse," leaving out but those particulars wherein they differ, and retaining only those wherein they agree, and of those making a new distinct complex idea, and giving the name "animal" to it, one has a more general term, that comprehends with man several other creatures.

The next thing therefore to be considered, is, what kind of signification it is that general words have. For as it is evident that they do not signify barely one particular thing, for then they would not be general terms, but proper names; so on the other side it is as evident they do not signify a plurality; for, "man" and "men" would then signify the same and the distinction of "numbers" (as grammarians call them) would be superfluous and useless. That then which general words signify, is a sort of things; and each of them does that by being a sign of an abstract idea in the mind; to which idea as things existing are found to agree, so they come to be ranked under that name; or which is all one, be of that sort. Whereby it is evident, that the essences of the sorts, or (if the Latin word pleases better) *species* of things, are nothing else but these abstract ideas. For the having the essence of any species, being that which makes anything to be of that species, and the conformity to the idea to which the name is annexed being that which gives a right to that name, the having the essence, and the having that conformity, must needs be the same thing: since to be of any species, and to have a right to the name of that species, is all one. As, for example: to be a man or of the species man, and to have right to the name "man" is the same thing. Again: to be a man, or of the species man, and have the essence of a man, is the same thing. Now, since nothing can be a man, or have a right to the name "man" but what has a conformity to the abstract idea the name "man" stands for; nor any thing be a man, or have a right to the species man, but what has the essence of that species; it follows, that the abstract idea for which the name stands, and the essence of the species, is one and the same. From whence it is easy to observe, that the essences of the sorts of things, and consequently the sorting of this, is the workmanship of the understanding that abstracts and makes those general ideas.

The common names of substances, as well as other general terms, stand for sorts: which is nothing else but the being made signs of such complex ideas, wherein several particular substances do or might agree, by virtue of which they are capable of being comprehended in one common conception, and be signified by one name.

The measure and boundary of each sort or species whereby it is constituted that particular sort and distinguished from others, is that we call its "essence," which is nothing but that abstract idea to which the name is annexed: so that everything contained in that idea is essential to that sort.

That "essence," in the ordinary use of the word, relates to sorts, and that it is considered in particular beings no farther than they are ranked into sorts, appears from hence: that take but away the abstract ideas by which we sort individuals, and rank them under common names, and then the thought of any thing essential to any of them instantly vanishes: we have no notion of the one without the other: which plainly shows their relation.

It is impossible therefore that any thing should determine the sorts of things which we rank under general names, but that idea which that name is designed as a mark for; which is that, as has been shown, which we call the "nominal essence." Why do we say, "This is a horse, and that a mule; this is an animal, that an herb?" How comes any particular thing to be of this or that sort, but because it has that nominal essence, or, which is all one, agrees to that abstract idea that name is annexed to? That our ranking and distinguishing natural substances into species, consists in the nominal essences the mind makes, and not in the real essences to be found in the things themselves, is farther evident from our ideas of spirits. For, the mind getting, only by reflecting on its own operations, those simple ideas which it attributes to spirits, it hath or can have no other notion of spirit but by attributing all those operations it finds in itself to a sort of beings, without consideration of matter.

Since, then, it is evident that we sort and name substances by their nominal, and not by their real, essences; the next thing to be considered is, how and by whom these essences come to be made. As to the latter, it is evident they are made by the mind, and not by nature: for were they nature's workmanship, they could not be so various and different in several men, as experience tells us they are. For if we will examine it, we shall not find the nominal essence of any one species of substance in all men the same; no, not of that which of all others we are the most intimately acquainted with.

But though these nominal essences of substances are made by the mind, they are not yet made so arbitrarily as those of mixed modes. To the making of any nominal essence, it is necessary, First, That the ideas whereof it consists, have such an union as to make but one idea, how compounded soever. Secondly, That the particular ideas so united be exactly the same, neither more nor less.

This, then, in short, is the case: nature makes many particular things which do agree one with another in many sensible qualities, and probably, too, in their internal frame and constitution; but it is not this real essence that distinguishes them into species; it is men, who taking occasion from the qualities they find united in them, and wherein they observe often several individuals to agree, range them into sorts in order to their naming, for the convenience of comprehensive signs; under which, individuals, according to their conformity to this or that abstract idea, come to be ranked as under ensigns; so that this is of the blue, that the red, regiment; this is a man, that a drill: and in this, I think, consists the whole business of *genus* and *species*.

ON KNOWLEDGE AND BELIEF.

Since the mind, in all its thoughts and reasonings, hath no other immediate object but its own ideas, which it alone does or can contemplate, it is evident that our knowledge is only conversant about them.

Knowledge then seems to me to be nothing but the perception of the connection and agreement, or disagreement and repugnancy, of any of our ideas. In this alone it consists. Where this perception is, there is knowledge; and where it is not, there, though we may fancy, guess, or believe, yet we always come short of knowledge.

But, to understand a little more distinctly wherein this agreement or disagreement consists, I think we may reduce it all to these four sorts : (1.) Identity, or diversity. (2.) Relation. (3.) Co-existence, or necessary connection. (4.) Real existence.

First, As to the first sort of agreement or disagreement, viz., identity or diversity. It is the first act of the mind, when it has any sentiments or ideas at all, to perceive its ideas, and, so far as it perceives them, to know each what it is, and thereby also to perceive their difference, and that one is not another. This is so absolutely necessary, that without it there could be no knowledge, no reasoning, no imagination, no distinct thoughts at all. This, then, is the first agreement or disagreement which the mind perceives in its ideas, which it always perceives at first sight; and if there ever happen any doubt about it, it will always be found to be about the names, and not the ideas themselves, whose identity and diversity will always be perceived as soon and as clearly as the ideas themselves are, nor can it possibly be otherwise.

Secondly, The next sort of agreement or disagreement the mind perceives in any of its ideas may, I think, be called "relative," and is nothing but the perception of the relation between any two ideas, of what kind soever, whether substances, modes, or any other. For, since all distinct ideas must eternally be known not to be the same, and so be universally and constantly denied one of another: there could be no room for any positive knowledge at all, if we could not perceive any relation between our ideas, and find out the agreement or disagreement they have one with another, in several ways the mind takes of comparing them.

Thirdly, The third sort of agreement or disagreement to be found in our ideas, which the perception of the mind is employed about, is co-existence, or non-co-existence in the same subject; and this belongs particularly to substances. Thus when we pronounce concerning "gold" that it is fixed, our knowledge of this truth amounts to no more but this, that fixedness, or a power to remain in the fire unconsumed, is an idea that always accompanies and is joined with that particular sort of yellowness, weight, fusibility, malleableness and solubility in *aqua regia*, which makes our complex idea, signified by the word "gold."

Fourthly, The fourth and last sort is that of actual real existence agreeing to any idea. Within these four sorts of agreement or disagreement is, I suppose, contained all the knowledge we have or are capable of; for, all the inquiries that we can make concerning any of our ideas, all that we know or can affirm concerning any of them, is, that it is or is not the same with some other; that it does or does not always co-exist with some other idea in the same subject; that it has this or that relation to some other idea; or that it has a real existence without the mind.

"What is truth?" was an inquiry many ages since; and it being that which all mankind either do or pretend to search after, it cannot but be worth our while carefully to examine wherein it consists; and so acquaint ourselves with the nature of it, as to observe how the mind distinguishes it from falsehood.

Truth then seems to me, in the proper import of the word, to signify nothing but the joining or separating of signs, as the things signified by them do agree or disagree one with another. The joining or separating of signs here meant, is what by another name we call "proposition."

When ideas are so put together or separated in the mind, as they or the things they stand for do agree or not, that is, as I may call it "mental truth." But truth of words is something more, and that is the affirming or denying of words one of another, as the ideas they stand for agree or disagree: and this again is twofold; either purely verbal or trifling, which I shall speak of (chap. x.) or real and instructive, which is the object of that real knowledge which we have spoken of already.

1. *The Degrees of Our Knowledge.*

All our knowledge consisting, as I have said, in the view the mind has of its own ideas, which is the utmost light and greatest certainty we, with our faculties and in our way of knowledge, are capable of, it may not be amiss to consider a little the degrees of its evidence. The different clearness of our knowledge seems to me to lie in the different way of perception the mind has of the agreement or disagreement of any of its ideas. For if we will reflect on our own ways of thinking, we shall find that sometimes the mind perceives the agreement or disagreement of two ideas immediately by themselves, without the intervention of any other : and this, I think, we may call "intuitive knowledge." For in this the mind is at no pains of proving or examining, but perceives the truth, as the eye doth light, only by being directed towards it. Thus the mind perceives that white is not black, that a circle is not a triangle ; that three are more than two, and equal to one and two. Such kind of truths the mind perceives at the first sight of the ideas together, by bare intuition, without the intervention of any other idea ; and this kind of knowledge is the clearest and most certain that human frailty is capable of. This part of knowledge is irresistible, and, like bright sunshine, forces itself immediately to be perceived as soon as ever the mind turns its view that way; and leaves no room for hesitation, doubt, or examination, but the mind is presently filled with the clear light of it. It is on this intuition that depends all the certainty and evidence of all our knowledge ; which certainty every one finds to be so great, that he cannot imagine, and therefore not require, a greater : for a man cannot conceive himself capable of a greater certainty, than to know that any idea in his mind is such as he perceives it to be : and that two ideas, wherein he perceives a difference, are different, and not precisely the same. He that demands a greater certainty than this demands he knows not what, and shows only that he has a mind to be a sceptic without being able to be so. Certainty depends so wholly on this intuition, that in the next degree of knowledge, which I call " demonstrative," this intuition is necessary in all the connections of the intermediate ideas, without which we cannot attain knowledge and certainty.

The next degree of knowledge is, where the mind perceives the agreement or disagreement of any ideas, but not immediately. Though wherever the mind perceives the agreement or disagreement of any of its ideas, there be certain knowledge ; yet it does not always happen that the mind sees that agreement or disagreement which there is between them, even where it is discoverable ; and in that case remains in ignorance, and at most gets no farther than a probable conjecture. The reason why the mind cannot always perceive presently the agreement or disagreement of two ideas, is, because those ideas concerning whose agreement or disagreement the inquiry is made, cannot by the mind be so put together as to show it. In this case then, when the mind cannot so bring its ideas together as, by their immediate comparison and, as it were, juxtaposition or application one to another, to perceive their agreement or disagreement, it is fain, by the intervention of other ideas (one or more, as it happens), to discover the agreement or disagreement which it searches ; and this is that which we call " reasoning."

Thus the mind, being willing to know the agreement or disagreement in bigness between the three angles of a triangle and two right ones, cannot, by an immediate view and comparing them, do it: because the three angles of a triangle cannot be brought at once, and be compared with any one or two angles; and so of this the mind has no immediate, no intuitive knowledge. In this case the mind is fain to find out some other angles, to which the three angles of a triangle have an equality; and finding those equal to two right ones, comes to know their equality to two right ones.

Those intervening ideas which serve to show the agreement of any two others, are called "proofs"; and where the agreement or disagreement is by this means plainly and clearly perceived, it is called "demonstration," it being shown to the understanding, and the mind made to see that it is so.

This knowledge by intervening proofs, though it be certain, yet the evidence of it is not altogether so clear and bright, nor the assent so ready, as in intuitive knowledge. For though in demonstration the mind does at last perceive the agreement or disagreement of the ideas it considers, yet it is not without pains and attention: there must be more than one transient view to find it.

Another difference between intuitive and demonstrative knowledge, is, that though in the latter all doubt be removed, when by the intervention of the intermediate ideas the agreement or disagreement is perceived; yet before the demonstration there was a doubt; which in intuitive knowledge cannot happen to the mind that has its faculty of perception left to a degree capable of distinct ideas, no more than it can be a doubt to the eye (that can distinctly see white and black), whether this ink and this paper be all of a color. If there be sight in the eyes, it will at first glimpse, without hesitation, perceive the words printed on this paper, different from the color of the paper.

Now, in every step reason makes in demonstrative knowledge, there is an intuitive knowledge of that agreement or disagreement it seeks with the next intermediate idea, which it uses as a proof : for if it were not so, that yet would need a proof ; since without the perception of such agreement or disagreement there is no knowledge produced. If it be perceived by itself, it is intuitive knowledge : if it cannot be perceived by itself, there is need of some intervening idea, as a common measure, to show their agreement or disagreement.

2. *The Extent of Human Knowledge.*

Knowledge, as has been said, lying in the perception of the agreement or disagreement of any of our ideas, it follows from hence, that,

— First, We can have knowledge no farther than we have ideas.

— Secondly, That we can have no knowledge farther than we can have perception of that agreement or disagreement : which perception being, (1.) Either by intuition, or the immediate comparing any two ideas ; o , (2.) By reason, examining the agreement or disagreement of two ideas by the intervention of some others ; or, (3.) By sensation, perceiving the existence of particular things : hence it also follows,

— Thirdly, That we cannot have an intuitive knowledge that shall extend itself to all our ideas, and all that we would know about them; because we cannot examine and perceive all the relations they have one to another by juxtaposition, or an immediate comparison one with another. Thus having the ideas of an obtuse and an acute angled triangle, both drawn from equal bases, and between parallels, I can by intuitive knowledge perceive the one not to be the other; but cannot that way know whether they be equal or no: because their agreement or disagreement in equality can never be perceived by an immediate comparing them; the difference of figure makes their parts uncapable of an exact immediate application; and therefore there is need of some intervening quantities to measure them by, which is demonstration or rational knowledge.

— Fourthly, It follows also, from what is above observed, that our rational knowledge cannot reach to the whole extent of our ideas: because between two different ideas we would examine, we cannot always find such mediums as we can connect one to another with an intuitive knowledge, in all the parts of the deduction; and wherever that fails, we come short of knowledge and demonstration.

— Fifthly, Sensitive knowledge, reaching no farther than the existence of things actually present to our senses, is yet much narrower than either of the former.

We have the ideas of matter and thinking, but possibly shall never be able to know whether any mere material being thinks or no; it being impossible for us, by the contemplation of our own ideas without revelation, to discover whether Omnipotency has not given to some systems of matter, fitly disposed, a power to perceive and think, or else joined and fixed to matter, so disposed, a thinking immaterial substance: it being, in respect of our notions, not much more remote from our comprehension to conceive that God can, if he pleases, superadd to matter a faculty of thinking, than that he should superadd to it another substance with a faculty of thinking; since we know not wherein thinking consists, nor to what sort of substances the Almighty has been pleased to give that power which cannot be in any created being but merely by the good pleasure and bounty of the Creator. For I see no contradiction in it, that the first eternal thinking Being should, if he pleased, give to certain systems of created senseless matter, put together as he thinks fit, some degrees of sense, perception, and thought: though, as I think I have proved, (lib. iv. chap. x.), it is no less than a contradiction to suppose matter (which is evidently in its own nature void of sense and thought) should be that eternal first thinking being. It is a point which seems to me to be put out of the reach of our knowledge: and he who will give himself leave to consider freely, and look into the dark and intricate part of each hypothesis, will scarce find his reason able to determine him fixedly for or against the soul's materiality; since on which side soever he views it, either as an unextended substance, or as a thinking extended matter, the difficulty to conceive either will, whilst either alone is in his thoughts, still drive him to the contrary side: an unfair way which some men take with themselves ; who, because of the unconceivableness of something they find in one, throw themselves violently into the contrary hypothesis, though altogether as unintelligible to an unbiassed understanding.

Secondly, As to the second sort, which is the agreement or disagreement of our ideas of co-existence, in this our knowledge is very short, though in this consists the greatest and most material part of our knowledge concerning substances. For our ideas of the species of substances being, as I have showed, nothing but certain collections of simple ideas united in one subject, and so co-existing together ;—*v. g.*, our idea of "flame" is a body hot, luminous, and moving upward ; of "gold," a body heavy to a certain degree, yellow, malleable, and fusible. These, or some such complex ideas as these in men's minds, do these two names of the different substances, "flame" and "gold," stand for. When we would know any thing farther concerning these, or any other sort of substances, what do we inquire but what other qualities or powers these substances have or have not? which is nothing else but to know what other simple ideas do or do not co-exist with those that make up that complex idea.

Our knowledge in all these inquiries reaches very little farther than our experience. Indeed some few of the primary qualities have a necessary dependence and visible connection one with another, as figure necessarily supposes extension, receiving or communicating motion by impulse supposes solidity. But though these and perhaps some others of our ideas have, yet there are so few of them that have, a visible connection one with another, that we can by intuition or demonstration discover the co-existence of very few of the qualities are to be found united in substances: and we are left only to the assistance of our senses to make known to us what qualities they contain. For, of all the qualities that are co-existent in any subject, without this dependence and evident connection of their ideas one with another, we cannot know certainly any two to co-exist any farther than experience, by our senses, informs us. Thus though we see the yellow color, and upon trial find the weight, malleableness, fusibility, and fixedness that are united in a piece of gold; yet, because no one of these ideas has any evident dependence or necessary connection with the other, we cannot certainly know that where any four of these are the fifth will be there also, how highly probable soever it may be: because the highest probability amounts not to certainty; without which there can be no true knowledge. For this co-existence can be no farther known than it is perceived: and it cannot be perceived but either in particular subjects by the observation of our senses, or in general by the necessary connection of the ideas themselves.

The names of substances, then, whenever made to stand for species which are supposed to be constituted by real essences which we know not, are not capable to convey certainty to the understanding: of the truth of general propositions made up of such terms we cannot be sure. The reason whereof is plain. For, how can we be sure that this or that quality is in gold, when we know not what is or is not gold? since in this way of speaking nothing is gold but what partakes of an essence, which we not knowing cannot know where it is or is not, and so cannot be sure that any parcel of matter in the world is or is not in this sense gold; being incurably ignorant whether it has or has not that which makes any thing to be called "gold," *i.e.*, that real essence of gold whereof we have no idea at all: this being as impossible for us to know, as it is for a blind man to tell in what flower the color of a pansy is or is not to be found, whilst he has no idea of the color of a pansy at all. Or if we could (which is impossible) certainly know where a real essence which we know not, is, *v. g.*, in what parcels of matter the real essence of gold is, yet could we not be sure that this or that quality could with truth be affirmed of gold: since it is impossible for us to know that this or that quality of idea has a necessary connection with a real essence, of which we have no idea at all, whatever species that supposed real essence may be imagined to constitute.

The complex ideas that our names of the species of substances properly stand for, are collections of such qualities as have been observed to co-exist in an unknown substratum which we call "substance;" but what other qualities necessarily co-exist with such combinations, we cannot certainly know, unless we can discover their natural dependence; which in their primary qualities we can go but a very little way in; and in all their secondary qualities we can discover no connection at all, for the reasons mentioned, (chap. iii.) viz., (1.) Because we know not the real constitutions of substances, on which each secondary quality particularly depends. (2.) Did we know that it would serve us only for experimental (not universal) knowledge; and reach with certainty no farther than that bare instance: because our understandings can discover no conceivable connection between any secondary quality, and any modification whatsoever of any of the primary ones. And therefore there are very few general propositions to be made concerning substances which can carry with them undoubted certainty.

And therefore I am apt to doubt, that how far soever human industry may advance useful and experimental philosophy in physical things, scientifical will still be out of our reach; because we want perfect and adequate ideas of those very bodies which are nearest to us, and most under our command. Those which we have ranked into classes under names, and we think ourselves best acquainted with, we have but very imperfect and incomplete ideas of. Distinct ideas of the several sorts of bodies that fall under the examination of our senses perhaps we may have; but adequate ideas, I suspect, we have not of any one amongst them.

"All gold is fixed," is a proposition whose truth we cannot be certain of, how universally soever it be believed. For if, according to the useless imagination of the Schools, any one supposes the term "gold" to stand for a species of things set out by nature by a real essence belonging to it, it is evident he knows not what particular substances are of that species; and so cannot, with certainty, affirm any thing universally of gold. For the chief part of our knowledge concerning substances is not, as in other things, barely of the relation of two ideas that may exist separately; but is of the necessary connection and co-existence of several distinct ideas in the same subject, or of their repugnances so to co-exist. Could we begin at the other end, and discover what it was therein that color consisted, what made a body lighter or heavier, what texture of parts made it malleable, fusible, and fixed, and fit to be dissolved in this sort of liquor, and not in another; if (I say) we had such an idea as this of bodies, and could perceive wherein all sensible qualities originally consist, and how they are produced, we might frame such abstract ideas of them as would furnish us with matter of more general knowledge, and enable us to make universal propositions that should carry general truth and certainty with them.

We are not therefore to wonder if certainty be to be found in very few general propositions made concerning substances; our knowledge of their qualities and properties go very seldom farther than our senses reach and inform us. Possibly inquisitive and observing men may, by strength of judgment, penetrate farther; and on probabilities taken from wary observation, and hints well laid together, often guess right at what experience has not yet discovered to them. But this is but guessing still; it amounts only to opinion, and has not that certainty which is requisite to knowledge. For all general knowledge lies only in our own thoughts, and consists barely in the contemplation of our own abstract ideas.

To conclude: general propositions, of what kind soever, are then only capable of certainty, when the terms used in them stand for such ideas whose agreement or disagreement as there expressed is capable to be discovered by us. And we are then certain of their truth or falsehood, when we perceive the ideas the terms stand for to agree or not agree, according as they are affirmed or denied one of another. Whence we may take notice, that general certainty is never to be found but in our ideas. Whenever we go to seek it elsewhere in experiment or observations without us, our knowledge goes not beyond particulars. It is the contemplation of our own abstract ideas that alone is able to afford us general knowledge.

If we are at a loss in respect of the powers and operations of bodies, I think it is easy to conclude we are much more in the dark in reference to spirits, whereof we naturally have no ideas but what we draw from that of our own, by reflecting on the operations of our own souls within us, as far as they can come within our observation. But how inconsiderable rank the spirits that inhabit our bodies hold amongst those various, and possibly innumerable, kinds of nobler beings; and how far short they come of the endowments and perfections of cherubims and seraphims, and infinite sorts of spirits above us, is what by a transient hint, in another place, I have offered to my reader's consideration.

As to the fourth sort of our knowledge, viz., of the real actual existence of things, we have an intuitive knowledge of our own existence; a demonstrative knowledge of the existence of a God; of the existence of any thing else, we have no other but a sensitive knowledge, which extends not beyond the objects present to our senses.

Our knowledge being so narrow, as I have showed, it will, perhaps, give us some light into the present state of our minds, if we look a little into the dark side, and take a view of our ignorance: which, being infinitely larger than our knowledge, may serve much to the quieting of disputes and improvement of useful knowledge, if, discovering how far we have clear and distinct ideas, we confine out thoughts within the contemplation of those things that are within the reach of our understandings, and launch not out into that abyss of darkness (where we have not eyes to see, nor faculties to perceive any thing), out of a presumption that nothing is beyond our comprehension.

We shall the less wonder to find it so when we consider the causes of our ignorance, which, from what has been said, I suppose, will be found to be chiefly these three:

FIRST, Want of ideas.

SECONDLY, Want of a discoverable connection between the ideas we have.

THIRDLY, Want of tracing and examining our ideas.

FIRST. There are some things, and those not a few, that we are ignorant of for want of ideas.

First. All the simple ideas we have are confined (as I have shown) to those we receive from corporeal objects by sensation, and from the operations of our own minds as the objects of reflection. But how much these few and narrow inlets are disproportionate to the vast whole extent of all beings, will not be hard to persuade those who are not so foolish as to think their span the measure of all things. What other simple ideas it is possible the creatures in other parts of the universe may have by the assistance of senses and faculties more or perfecter than we have, or different from ours, it is not for us to determine; but to say or think there are no such because we conceive nothing of them, is no better an argument than if a blind man should be positive in it, that there was no such thing as sight and colors because he had no manner of idea of any such thing, nor could by any means frame to himself any notions about seeing.

Secondly, Another great cause of ignorance is the want of ideas we are capable of. As the want of ideas which our faculties are not able to give us shuts us wholly from those views of things which it is reasonable to think other beings, perfecter than we, have, of which we know nothing; so the want of ideas I now speak of keeps us in ignorance of things we conceive capable of being known to us. Bulk, figure, and motion, we have ideas of. But though we are not without ideas of these primary qualities of bodies in general, yet not knowing what is the particular bulk, figure, and motion of the greatest part of the bodies of the universe, we are ignorant of the several powers, efficacies, and ways of operation, whereby the effects which we daily see are produced. These are hid from us in some things by being too remote; and, in others, by being too minute.

I doubt not but if we could discover the figure, size, texture, and motion of the minute constituent parts of any two bodies, we should know without trial several of their operations one upon another, as we do now the properties of a square or a triangle. Did we know the mechanical affections of the particles of rhubarb, hemlock, opium, and a man, as a watchmaker does those of a watch, whereby it performs its operations, and of a file, which, by rubbing on them, will alter the figure of any of the wheels, we should be able to tell beforehand that rhubarb will purge, hemlock kill, and opium make a man sleep, as well as a watchmaker can, that a little piece of paper laid on the balance will keep the watch from going till it be removed; or that some small part of it being rubbed by a file, the machine would quite lose its motion, and the watch go no more.

SECONDLY, What a small part of the substantial beings that are in the universe the want of ideas leaves open to our knowledge, we have seen. In the next place, another cause of ignorance of no less moment is a want of a discoverable connection between those ideas which we have. For wherever we want that, we are utterly uncapable of universal and certain knowledge; and are, as in the former case, left only to observation and experiment; which how narrow and confined it is, how far from general knowledge, we need not be told. I shall give some few instances of this cause of our ignorance, and so leave it. It is evident that the bulk, figure, and motion of several bodies about us, produce in us several sensations, as of colors, sounds, taste, smell, pleasure, and pain, etc. These mechanical affections of bodies having no affinity at all with those ideas they produce in us (there being no conceivable connexion between any impulse of any sort of body, and any perception of a color or smell which we find in our minds), we can have no distinct knowledge of such operations beyond our experience; and can reason no otherwise about them than as effects produced by the appointment of an infinitely wise Agent, which perfectly surpass our comprehensions.

3. *The Reality of Our Knowledge.*

Wherever we perceive the agreement or disagreement of any of our ideas, there is certain knowledge: and wherever we are sure those ideas agree with the reality of things, there is certain real knowledge.

It is evident the mind knows not things immediately, but only by the intervention of the ideas it has of them. Our knowledge therefore is real only so far as there is a conformity between our ideas and the reality of things. But what shall be here the criterion? How shall the mind, when it perceives nothing but its own ideas, know that they agree with things themselves? This, though it seems not to want difficulty, yet I think there be two sorts of ideas that we may be assured agree with things:

First. The first are simple ideas, which since the mind, as has been shown, can by no means make to itself, must necessarily be the product of things operating on the mind in the natural way, and producing therein those perceptions which by the wisdom and will of our Maker they are ordained and adapted to. From whence it follows, that simple ideas are not fictions of our fancies, but the natural and regular productions of things without us really operating upon us; and so carry with them all the conformity which is intended, or which our state requires; for they represent to us things under those appearances which they are fitted to produce in us, whereby we are enabled to distinguish the sorts of particular substances, to discern the states they are in, and so to take them for our necessities, and apply them to our uses. Thus the idea of whiteness or bitterness, as it is in the mind, exactly answering that power which is in any body to produce it there, has all the real conformity it can or ought to have with things without us. And this conformity between our simple ideas and the existence of things is sufficient for real knowledge.

Secondly. All our complex ideas except those of substances being archetypes of the mind's own making, not intended to be the copies of any thing, nor referred to the existence of any thing, as to their originals, cannot want any conformity necessary to real knowledge.

We can know then the truth of two sorts of propositions with perfect certainty; the one is, of those trifling propositions which have a certainty in them, but it is only a verbal certainty, but not instructive. And, secondly, we can know the truth, and so may be certain in propositions which affirm something of another, which is a necessary consequence of its precise complex idea, but not contained in it: as that "the external angle of all triangles is bigger than either of the opposite internal angles;" which relation of the outward angle to either of the opposite internal angles, making no part of the complex idea signified by the name "triangle," this is a real truth, and conveys with it instructive real knowledge.

I doubt not but it will be easily granted that the knowledge we have of mathematical truths, is not only certain, but real knowledge; and not the bare empty vision of vain, insignificant chimeras of the brain: and yet, if we will consider, we shall find that it is only of our own ideas. The mathematician considers the truth and properties belonging to a rectangle or circle, only as they are in idea in his own mind. For it is possible he never found either of them existing mathematically, *i. e.*, precisely true in his life. But yet the knowledge he has of any truths or properties belonging to a circle, or any other mathematical figure, are nevertheless true and certain even of real things existing: because real things are no farther concerned, nor intended to be meant by any such propositions, than as things really agree to those archetypes in his mind.

And hence it follows that moral knowledge is as capable of real certainty as mathematics. For, certainty being but the perception of the agreement or disagreement of our ideas, and demonstration nothing but the perception of such agreement by the intervention of other ideas or mediums, our moral ideas as well as mathematical being archetypes themselves, and so adequate and complete ideas, all the agreement or disagreement which we shall find in them will produce real knowledge, as well as in mathematical figures.

Let us proceed now to inquire concerning our knowledge of the existence of things, and how we come by it. I say then, that we have the knowledge of our own existence by intuition; of the existence of God by demonstration; and of other things by sensation.

As for our own existence, we perceive it so plainly and so certainly that it neither needs nor is capable of any proof. For nothing can be more evident to us than our own existence. I think, I reason, I feel pleasure and pain : can any of these be more evident to me than my own existence? If I doubt of all things, that very doubt makes me perceive my own existence, and will not suffer me to doubt of that. For, if I know I feel pain, it is evident I have as certain perception of my own existence, as of the existence of the pain I feel : or if I know I doubt, I have as certain perception of the existence of the thing doubting, as of that thought which I call "doubt." Experience, then, convinces us that we have an intuitive knowledge of our own existence, and an internal infallible perception that we are. In every act of sensation, reasoning, or thinking, we are conscious to ourselves of our own being ; and, in this matter, come not short of the highest degree of certainty.

Though God has given us no innate ideas of himself ; though he has stamped no original characters on our minds, wherein we may read his being ; yet, having furnished us with those faculties our minds are endowed with, he hath not left himself without witness ; since we have sense, perception, and reason, and cannot want a clear proof of him as long as we carry ourselves about us. To show, therefore, that we are capable of knowing, *i. e.*, being certain, that there is a God, and how we may come by this certainty, I think we may go no farther than ourselves, and that undoubted knowledge we have of our own existence.

I think it is beyond question, that man has a clear

perception of his own being; he knows certainly that he exists, and that he is something. This, then, I think I may take for a truth, which every one's certain knowledge assures him of beyond the liberty of doubting, viz., that he is something that actually exists.

In the next place, man knows by an intuitive certainty that bare nothing can no more produce any real being, than it can be equal to two right angles. If a man knows not that nonentity, or the absence of all being, cannot be equal to two right angles, it is impossible he should know any demonstration in Euclid. If therefore we know there is some real being, and that nonentity cannot produce any real being, it is an evident demonstration, that from eternity there has been something; since what was not from eternity had a beginning; and what had a beginning must be produced by something else.

Next, it is evident, that what had its being and beginning from another, must also have all that which is in and belongs to its being from another too. All the powers it has, must be owing to and received from the same source. This eternal source, then, of all being, must also be the source and original of all power: and so this Eternal Being must be also the most powerful.

Again: a man finds in himself perception and knowledge. We have then got one step farther; and we are certain now that there is not only some being, but some knowing, intelligent being in the world.

There was a time, then, when there was no knowing being, and when knowledge began to be; or else there has been also a knowing Being from eternity. If it be said, "There was a time when no being had any knowledge, when that Eternal Being was void of all understanding;" I reply, that then it was impossible there should ever have been any knowledge; it being as impossible that things wholly void of knowledge, and operating blindly and without any perception, should produce a knowing being, as it is impossible that a triangle should make itself three angles bigger than two right ones. For it is as repugnant to the idea of senseless matter that it should put into itself sense-perception, and knowledge, as it is repugnant to the idea of a triangle that it should put into itself greater angles than two right ones.

Thus from the consideration of ourselves, and what we infallibly find in our own constitutions, our reason leads us to the knowledge of this certain and evident truth, that there is an eternal, most powerful, and most knowing Being, which whether any one will please to call "God," it matters not. The thing is evident; and from this idea duly considered, will easily be deducted all those other attributes which we ought to ascribe to this Eternal Being. Though our own being furnishes us, as I have shown, with an evident and incontestable proof of a Deity; and I believe nobody can avoid the cogency of it who will but as carefully attend to it as to any other demonstration of so many parts; yet this being so fundamental a truth, and of that consequence that all religion and genuine morality depend thereon, I doubt not but I shall be forgiven by my reader if I go over some parts of this argument again, and enlarge a little more upon them.

There is no truth more evident than that something must be from eternity.

It being then unavoidable for all rational creatures to conclude that something has existed from eternity, let us next see what kind of thing that must be.

There are but two sorts of beings in the world that man knows or conceives :—

First, Such as are purely material, without sense, perception, or thought, as the clippings of our beards and parings of our nails.

Secondly, Sensible, thinking, perceiving beings, such as we find ourselves to be ; which, if you please, we will hereafter call "cogitative and incogitative beings ;" which to our present purpose, if for nothing else, are perhaps better terms than "material and immaterial."

If then there must be something eternal, let us see what sort of being it must be. And to that it is very obvious to reason, that it must necessarily be a cogitative being. For it is as impossible to conceive that ever bare incogitative matter should produce a thinking intelligent being, as that nothing should of itself produce matter.

I appeal to every one's own thoughts, whether he cannot as easily conceive matter produced by nothing, as thought to be produced by pure matter, when before there was no such thing as thought or an intelligent being existing. If matter were the eternal first cogitative being, there would not be one eternal infinite cogitative being, but an infinite number of eternal finite cogitative beings independent one of another, of limited force and distinct thoughts, which could never produce that order, harmony, and beauty, which is to be found in nature. Since, therefore, whatsoever is the first eternal being must necessarily be cogitative; and whatsoever is first of all things must necessarily contain in it, and actually have, at least, all the perfections that can ever after exist; nor can it ever give to another any perfection that it hath not, either actually in itself or at least in a higher degree: it necessarily follows, that the first eternal being cannot be matter.

If, therefore, it be evident that something necessarily must exist from eternity, it is also as evident that that something must necessarily be a cogitative being: for it is as impossible that incogitative matter should produce a cogitative being, as that nothing, or the negation of all being, should produce a positive being or matter.

The knowledge of our own being we have by intuition. The existence of a God reason clearly makes known to us, as has been shown.

The knowledge of the existence of any other thing, we can have only by sensation: for, there being no necessary connection of real existence with any idea a man hath in his memory, nor of any other existence but that of God with the existence of any particular man, no particular man can know the existence of any other being, but only when by actual operating upon him it makes itself perceived by him. For, the having the idea of any thing in our mind no more proves the existence of that thing than the picture of a man evidences his being in the world, or the visions of a dream make thereby a true history.

It is therefore the actual receiving of ideas from without that gives us notice of the existence of other things, and makes us know that something doth exist at that time without us which causes that idea in us, though perhaps we neither know nor consider how it does it: for it takes not from the certainty of our senses, and the ideas we receive by them, that we know not the manner wherein they are produced; *v. g.*, whilst I write this, I have, by the paper affecting my eyes, that idea produced in my mind which whatever object causes, I call "white;" by which I know that that quality or accident (*i. e.*, whose appearance before my eyes always causes that idea) doth really exist and hath a being without me.

The notice we have by our senses of the existing of things without us, though it be not altogether so certain as our intuitive knowledge, or the deductions of our reason employed about the clear abstract ideas of our own minds; yet it is an assurance that deserves the name of knowledge. If we persuade ourselves that our faculties act and inform us right concerning the existence of those objects that affect them, it cannot pass for an ill-grounded confidence: for I think nobody can, in earnest, be so sceptical as to be uncertain of the existence of those things which he sees and feels.

This is certain, the confidence that our faculties do not herein deceive us is the greatest assurance we are capable of concerning the existence of material beings. For we cannot act any thing but by our faculties, nor talk of knowledge itself but by the help of those faculties which are fitted to apprehend even what knowledge is. But, besides the assurance we have from our senses themselves, that they do not err in the information they give us of the existence of things without us, when they are affected by them, we are farther confirmed in this assurance by other concurrent reasons.

First, It is plain those perceptions are produced in us by exterior causes affecting our senses, because those that want the organs of any sense never can have the ideas belonging to that sense produced in their minds.

Secondly, Because sometimes I find that I cannot avoid the having those ideas produced in my mind; for though when my eyes are shut, or windows fast, I can at pleasure recall to my mind the ideas of light or the sun, which former sensations had lodged in my memory; so I can at pleasure lay by that idea, and take into my view that of the smell of a rose, or taste of sugar. But if I turn my eyes at noon towards the sun, I cannot avoid the ideas which the light or sun then produces in me. So that there is a manifest difference between the ideas laid up in my memory (over which, if they were there only, I should have constantly the same power to dispose of them, and lay them by at pleasure), and those which force themselves upon me and I cannot avoid having. And therefore it must needs be some exterior cause, and the brisk acting of some objects without me, whose efficacy I cannot resist, that produces those ideas in my mind, whether I will or no.

Fourthly, Our senses, in many cases, bear witness to the truth of each other's report concerning the existence of sensible things without us. He that sees a fire may, if he doubt whether it be any thing more than a bare fancy, feel it too, and be convinced by putting his hand in it; which certainly could never be put into such exquisite pain by a bare idea or phantom, unless that the pain be a fancy too: which yet he cannot, when the burn is well, by raising the idea of it, bring upon himself again.

So that this evidence is as great as we can desire, being as certain to us as our pleasure or pain, *i.e.*, happiness or misery; beyond which we have no concernment either of knowing or being. Such an assurance of the existence of things without us, is sufficient to direct us in the attaining the good and avoiding the evil which is caused by them, which is the important concernment we have of being made acquainted with them.

In fine, then, when our senses do actually convey into our understandings any idea, we cannot but be satisfied that there doth something at that time really exist without us which doth affect our senses, and by them give notice of itself to our apprehensive faculties, and actually produce that idea which we then perceive: and we cannot so far distrust their testimony as to doubt that such collections of simple ideas as we have observed by our senses to be united together, do really exist together. But this knowledge extends as far as the present testimony of our senses, employed about particular objects that do then affect them, and no farther. For if I saw such a collection of simple ideas as is wont to be called "man" existing together one minute since, and am now alone; I cannot be certain that the same man exists now, since there is no necessary connection of his existence a minute since, with his existence now : by a thousand ways he may cease to be, since I had the testimony of my senses for his existence.

As, when our senses are actually employed about any object, we do not know that it does exist, so by our memory we may be assured that heretofore things that affected our senses have existed. And thus we have knowledge of the past existence of several things, whereof our senses having informed us, our memories still retain the ideas ; and of this we are past all doubt so long as we remember well. But this knowledge also reaches no farther than our senses have formerly assured us.

Of Judgment and Probability.

The understanding faculties being given to man, not barely for speculation, but also for the conduct of his life, man would be at a great loss if he had nothing to direct him but what has the certainty of true knowledge. For, that being very short and scanty, as we have seen, he would be often utterly in the dark, and in most of the actions of his life perfectly at a stand, had he nothing to guide him in the absence of clear and certain knowledge. He that will not eat till he has demonstration that it will nourish him, he that will not stir till he infallibly knows the business he goes about will succeed, will have little else to do but sit still and perish.

The faculty which God has given man to supply the want of clear and certain knowledge, in cases where that cannot be had, is judgment : whereby the mind takes its ideas to agree or disagree ; or, which is the same, any proposition to be true or false, without perceiving a demonstrative evidence in the proofs.

This faculty of the mind, when it is exercised immediately about things, is called "judgment ;" when about truths delivered in words, is most commonly called "assent" or "dissent :" which being the most usual way wherein the mind has occasion to employ this faculty, I shall, under these terms, treat of it as least liable in our language to equivocation.

Thus the mind has two faculties conversant about truth and falsehood,—

First, Knowledge, whereby it certainly perceives, and is undoubtedly satisfied of the agreement or disagreement of any ideas.

Secondly, Judgment, which is the putting ideas together, or separating them from one another in the mind, when their certain agreement or disagreement is not perceived, but presumed to be so ; which is, as the word imports, taken to be so before it certainly appears. And if it so unites or separates them as in reality things are, it is right judgment.

As demonstration is the showing the agreement or disagreement of two ideas by the intervention of one or more proofs, which have a constant, immutable, and visible connection one with another ; so probability is nothing but the appearance of such an agreement or disagreement by the intervention of proofs, whose connection is not constant and immutable, or at least is not perceived to be so ; but is, or appears for the most part to be so, and is enough to induce the mind to judge the proposition to be true or false, rather than the contrary.

Probability is likeliness to be true; the very notation of the word signifying such a proposition for which there be arguments or proofs to make it pass, or be received, for true. The entertainment the mind gives this sort of propositions is called "belief," "assent," or "opinion," which is the admitting or receiving any proposition for true, upon arguments or proofs that are found to persuade us to receive it as true, without certain knowledge that it is so. And herein lies the difference between probability and certainty, faith and knowledge, that in all the parts of knowledge there is intuition; each immediate idea, each step, has its visible and certain connection: in belief not so. That which makes me believe, is something extraneous to the thing I believe; something not evidently joined on both sides to, and so not manifestly showing the agreement or disagreement of those ideas that are under consideration.

Probability, then, being to supply the defect of our knowledge, and to guide us where that fails, is always conversant about propositions whereof we have no certainty, but only some inducements to receive them for true. The grounds of it are, in short, these two following:

First. The conformity of any thing with our own knowledge, observation, and experience.

Secondly. The testimony of others, vouching their observation and experience. In the testimony of others, is to be considered, (1.) The number. (2.) The integrity. (3.) The skill of the witnesses. (4.)

The design of the author, where it is a testimony out of a book cited. (5.) The consistency of the parts and circumstances of the relation. (6.) Contrary testimonies.

Upon these grounds depends the probability of any proposition : and as the conformity of our knowledge, as the certainty of observations, as the frequency and constancy of experience, and the number and credibility of testimonies do more or less agree or disagree with it, so is any proposition in itself more or less probable.

The grounds of probability we have laid down in the foregoing chapter, as they are the foundations on which our assent is built, so are they also the measure whereby its several degrees are or ought to be regulated : only we are to take notice, that whatever grounds of probability there may be, they yet operate no further on the mind, which searches after truth and endeavors to judge right, than they appear at least in the first judgment or search that the mind makes.

But, to return to the grounds of assent, and the several degrees of it : we are to take notice that the propositions we receive upon inducements of probability are of two sorts ; either concerning some particular existence, or, as it is usually termed, "matter-of-fact," which, falling under observation, is capable of human testimony ; or else concerning things which, being beyond the discovery of our senses, are not capable of any such testimony.

Concerning the first of these, viz., particular matter-of-fact :—

First, Where any particular thing, consonant to the constant observation of ourselves and others in the like case, comes attested by the concurrent reports of all that mention it, we receive it as easily and build as firmly upon it as if it were certain knowledge ; and we reason and act thereupon with as little doubt as if it were.

The first, therefore, and highest degree of probability is, when the general consent of all men in all ages, as far as it can be known, concurs with a man's constant and never-failing experience in like cases, to confirm the truth of any particular matter-of-fact attested by fair witnesses ; such are all the stated constitutions and properties of bodies, and the regular proceedings of causes and effects in the ordinary course of nature.

Secondly, The next degree of probability is, when I find by my own experience, and the agreement of all orders that mention it, a thing to be for the most part so ; and that the particular instance of it is attested by many and undoubted witnesses ; *v. g.*, history giving us such an account of men in all ages, and my own experience, as far as I had an opportunity to observe, confirming it, that most men prefer their private advantage to the public ; if all historians that write of Tiberius say, that Tiberius did so, it is extremely probable. And in this case, our assent has a sufficient foundation to raise itself to a degree which we may call " confidence."

Thirdly, In things that happen indifferently, as "that a bird should fly this or that way," "that it should thunder on a man's right or left hand," etc., when any particular matter-of-fact is vouched by the concurrent testimony of unsuspected witnesses, there our assent is also unavoidable.

The difficulty is, when testimonies contradict common experience, and the reports of history and witnesses clash with the ordinary course of nature, or with one another; there it is where diligence, attention, and exactness is required to form a right judgment, and to proportion the assent to the different evidence and probability of the thing, which rises and falls according as those two foundations of credibility, viz., common observation in like cases, and particular testimonies in that particular instance, favor or contradict it.

The probabilities we have hitherto mentioned are only such as concern matter-of-fact, and such things as are capable of observation and testimony. There remains that other sort concerning which men entertain opinions with variety of assent, though the things be such that, falling not under the reach of our senses, they are not capable of testimony. Such are, (1.) The existence, nature, and operations of finite immaterial beings without us, as spirits, angels, devils, etc., or the existence of material beings, which, either from their smallness in themselves or remoteness from us, our senses cannot take notice of: as whether there be any plants, animals, and intelligent inhabitants in the planets and other mansions of the vast universe. (2) Concerning the manner of operation in most parts of the works of nature; wherein, though we see the sensible effects, yet their causes are unknown, and we perceive not the ways and manner how they are produced.

Though the common experience and the ordinary course of things have justly a mighty influence on the minds of men to make them give or refuse credit to any thing proposed to their belief; yet there is one case wherein the strangeness of the fact lessens not the assent to a fair testimony given of it. For, where such supernatural events are suitable to ends aimed at by Him who has the power to change the course of nature, there, under such circumstances, they may be the fitter to procure belief, by how much the more they are beyond or contrary to ordinary observation. This is the proper case of miracles; which, well attested, do not only find credit themselves, but give it also to other truths which need such confirmation.

Besides those we have hitherto mentioned, there is one sort of propositions that challenge the highest degree of our assent, upon bare testimony, whether the thing proposed agree or disagree with common experience and the ordinary course of things or no. The reason whereof is, because the testimony is of such an one as cannot deceive nor be deceived, and that is of God himself. This carries with it assurance beyond doubt, evidence beyond exception. This is called by a peculiar name, "revelation," and our assent to it, "faith;" which as absolutely determines our minds and as perfectly excludes all wavering, as our knowledge itself: and we may as well doubt of our own being as we can whether any revelation from God be true.

REASON AND REASONING.

If general knowledge, as has been shown, consists in a perception of the agreement or disagreement of our own ideas, and the knowledge of the existence of all things without us (except only of a God, whose existence every man may certainly know and demonstrate to himself from his own existence) be had only by our senses; what room then is there for the exercise of any other faculty but outward sense and inward perception? What need is there of reason? Very much; both for the enlargement of our knowledge and regulating our assent: for it hath to do both in knowledge and opinion, and is necessary and assisting to all our other intellectual faculties, and indeed contains two of them, viz., sagacity and illation. By the one it finds out, and by the other it so orders, the intermediate ideas as to discover what connection there is in each link of the chain, whereby the extremes are held together; and thereby, as it were, to draw into view the truth sought for, which is that we call "illation" or "inference," and consists in nothing but the perception of the connection there is between the ideas in each step of the deduction, whereby the mind comes to see either the certain agreement or disagreement of any two ideas, as in demonstration, in which it arrives at knowledge; or their probable connection, on which it gives or withholds its assent, as in opinion. Sense and intuition reach but a very little way. The greatest part of our knowledge depends upon deductions and intermediate ideas: and in those cases where we are fain to substitute assent instead of knowledge, and take propositions for true without being certain they are so, we have need to find out, examine, and compare the grounds of their probability. In both these cases the faculty which finds out the means, and rightly applies them to discover certainty in the one and probability in the other, is that which we call " reason." For, as reason perceives the necessary and indubitable connection of all the ideas or proofs one to another in each step of any demonstration that produces knowledge, so it likewise perceives the probable connection of all the ideas or proofs one to another, in every step of a discourse to which it will think assent due. This is the lowest degree of that which can be truly called "reason." For, where the mind does not perceive this probable connection, where it does not discern whether there be any such connection or no, there men's opinions are not the product of judgment or the consequence of reason, but the effects of chance and hazard, of a mind floating at all adventures, without choice and without direction.

So that we may in reason consider these four degrees: The first and highest is the discovering and finding out of proofs; the second, the regular and methodical disposition of them, and laying them in a clear and fit order, to make their connection and force be plainly and easily perceived; the third is the perceiving their connection; and the fourth, a making a right conclusion. These several degrees may be observed in any mathematical demonstration: it being one thing, to perceive the connection of each part as the demonstration is made by another; another, to perceive the dependence of the conclusion on all the parts; a third, to make out a demonstration clearly and neatly one's self; and something different from all these, to have first found out those intermediate ideas or proofs by which it is made.

There is one thing more which I shall desire to be considered concerning reason; and that is, whether syllogism, as is generally thought, be the proper instrument of it, and the usefullest way of exercising this faculty. The causes I have no doubt are these:—

First, Because syllogism serves our reason but in one only of the fore-mentioned parts of it; and that is, to show the connection of the proofs in any one instance and no more; but in this it is of no great use, since the mind can perceive such connection, where it really is as easily, nay perhaps better, without it.

If we will observe the actings of our own minds, we shall find that we reason best and clearest when we only observe the connection of the proof, without reducing our thoughts to any rule of syllogism. And therefore we may take notice that there are many men that reason exceeding clear and rightly, who know not how to make a syllogism.

But God has not been so sparing to men to make them barely two-legged creatures, and left it to Aristotle to make them rational; *i. e.*, those few of them that he could get so to examine the grounds of syllogisms as to see that in above threescore ways that three propositions may be laid together, there are but about fourteen wherein one may be sure that the conclusion is right, and upon what ground it is that in these few the conclusion is certain, and in the other not. God has been more bountiful to mankind than so; he has given them a mind that can reason without being instructed in methods of syllogism: the understanding is not taught to reason by these rules; it has a native faculty to perceive the coherence or incoherence of its ideas and can range them right without any such perplexing repetitions.

Inference is looked on as the great act of the rational faculty; and so it is when it is rightly made: but the mind, either very desirous to enlarge its knowledge, or very apt to favor the sentiments it has once imbibed, is very forward to make inferences, and therefore often makes too much haste before it perceives the connection of the ideas that must hold the extremes together.

To infer is nothing but, by virtue of one proposition laid down as true, to draw in another as true; *i. e.*, to see or suppose such a connection of the two ideas of the inferred proposition. *V. g.*, let this be the proposition laid down, "Men shall be punished in another world," and from thence be inferred this other, "Then men can determine themselves." The question now is to know whether the mind has made this inference right or no; if it has made it by finding out the intermediate ideas, and taking a view of the connection of them placed in a due order, it has proceeded rationally, and made a right inference. If it has done it without such a view, it has not so much made an inference that will hold, or an inference of right reason, as shown a willingness to have it be or be taken for such. But in neither case is it syllogism that discovered those ideas, or showed the connection of them; for they must be both found out, and the connection everywhere perceived, before they can rationally be made use of in syllogism.

Another reason that makes me doubt whether syllogism be the only proper instrument of reason in the discovery of truth, is, that of whatever use mode and figure is pretended to be in the laying open of fallacy (which has been above considered), those scholastic forms of discourse are not less liable to fallacies than the plainer ways of argumentation; and for this I appeal to common observation, which has always found these artificial methods of reasoning more adapted to catch and entangle the mind than to instruct and inform the understanding.

The rules of syllogism serve not to furnish the mind with those intermediate ideas that may show the connection of remote ones. This way of reasoning discovers no new proofs, but is the art of marshalling and ranging the old ones we have already. The forty-seventh proposition of the first book of Euclid is very true; but the discovery of it, I think, not owing to any rules of common logic. A man knows first, and then he is able to prove syllogistically: so that syllogism comes after knowledge; and then a man has little or no need of it.

It is fit before I leave this subject, to take notice of one manifest mistake in the rules of syllogism; viz., "that no syllogistical reasoning can be right and conclusive but what has, at least, one general proposition in it;" as if we could not reason and have knowledge about particulars : whereas, in truth, the matter rightly considered, the immediate object of all our reasoning and knowledge is nothing but particulars. Every man's reasoning and knowledge is only about the ideas existing in his own mind, which are truly, every one of them, particular existences ; and our knowledge and reasoning about other things is only as they correspond with those our particular ideas. So that the perception of the agreement or disagreement of our particular ideas, is the whole and utmost of all our knowledge. Universality is but accidental to it, and consists only in this, that the particular ideas about which it is are such as more than one particular thing can correspond with and be represented by. But the perception of the agreement or disagreement of any two ideas, and consequently our knowledge, is equally clear and certain, whether either, or both, or neither of those ideas be capable of representing more real beings than one, or no.

Faith and Reason.

It has been above shown, (1.) That we are of necessity ignorant, and want knowledge of all sorts where we want ideas. (2.) That we are ignorant, and want rational knowledge where we want proofs. (3.) That we want general knowledge and certainty as far as we want clear and determined specific ideas. (4.) That we want probability to direct our assent in matters where we have neither knowledge of our own nor testimony of other men to bottom our reason upon.

From these things thus premised, I think we may come to lay down the measures and boundaries between faith and reason; the want whereof may possibly have been the cause, if not of great disorders, yet at least of great disputes, and perhaps mistakes, in the world.

I think it may not be amiss to take notice, that, however faith be opposed to reason, faith is nothing but a firm assent of the mind; which, if it be regulated, as is our duty, cannot be afforded to any thing but upon good reason, and so cannot be opposite to it. He that believes without having any reason for believing, may be in love with his own fancies; but neither seeks truth as he ought, nor pays the obedience due to his Maker, who would have him use those discerning faculties he has given him to keep him out of mistake and error. He that does not this to the best of his power, however he sometimes lights on truth, is in the right but by chance; and I know not whether the luckiness of the accident will excuse the irregularity of his proceeding.

Reason therefore here, as contradistinguished to faith, I take to be the discovery of the certainty or probability of such propositions or truths which the mind arrives at by deduction made from such ideas which it has got by the use of its natural faculties, viz., by sensation or reflection.

Faith, on the other side, is the assent to any proposition, not thus made out by the deductions of reason, but upon the credit of the proposer, as coming from God in some extraordinary way of communication.

This way of discovering truths to men we call "revelation."

Whatsoever truth we come to the clear discovery of, from the knowledge and contemplation of our own ideas, will always be certainer to us than those which are conveyed to us by traditional revelation: for the knowledge we have that this revelation came at first from God, can never be so sure as the knowledge we have from the clear and distinct perception of the agreement or disagreement of our own ideas: *v. g.*, if it were revealed some ages since, that the three angles of a triangle were equal to two right ones, I might assent to the truth of that proposition upon the credit of the tradition that it was revealed: but that would never amount to so great a certainty as the knowledge of it upon the comparing and measuring my own ideas of two right angles, and the three angles of a triangle. The like holds in matter-of-fact, knowable by our senses: *v. g.*, the history of the deluge is conveyed to us by writings which had their original from revelation; and yet nobody, I think, will say he has as certain and clear a knowledge of the flood as Noah, that saw it, or that he himself would have had, had he then been alive and seen it. For he has no greater an assurance than that of his senses, that it is writ in the book supposed writ by Moses inspired: but he has not so great an assurance that Moses writ that book as if he had seen Moses write it. So that the assurance of its being a revelation is less still than the assurance of his senses.

In propositions, then, whose certainty is built upon the clear perception of the agreement or disagreement of our ideas, attained either by immediate intuition, as in self-evident propositions, or by evident deductions of reason in demonstrations, we need not the assistance of revelation as necessary to gain our assent and introduce them into our minds; because the natural ways of knowledge could settle them there, or had done it already, which is the greatest assurance we can possibly have of any thing, unless where God immediately reveals it to us; and thereto our assurance can be no greater than our knowledge is, that it is a revelation from God. But yet nothing, I think, can under that title shake or overrule plain knowledge, or rationally prevail with any man to admit it for true, in a direct contradiction to the clear evidence of his own understanding.

For since no evidence of our faculties by which we receive such revelations can exceed, if equal, the certainty of our intuitive knowledge, we can never receive for a truth any thing that is directly contrary to our clear and distinct knowledge. And therefore no proposition can be received for divine revelation, or obtain the assent due to all such, if it be contradictory to our clear intuitive knowledge, because this would be to subvert the principles and foundations of all knowledge, evidence, and assent whatsoever: and there would be left no difference between truth and falsehood, no measures of credible and incredible in the world, if doubtful propositions shall take place before self-evident, and what we certainly know give way to what we may possibly be mistaken in.

Whatever God hath revealed is certainly true; no doubt can be made of it. This is the proper object of faith : but whether it be a divine revelation or no, reason must judge ; which can never permit the mind to reject a greater evidence to embrace what is less evident, nor allow it to entertain probability in opposition to knowledge and certainty. There can be no evidence that any traditional revelation is of divine original, in the words we receive it, and in the sense we understand it, so clear and so certain as that of the principles of reason : and therefore nothing that is contrary to, and inconsistent with, the clear and self-evident dictates of reason has a right to be urged or assented to as a matter of faith, wherein reason hath nothing to do. Whatsoever is divine revelation ought to over-rule all our opinions, prejudices, and interests, and hath a right to be received with full assent : such a submission as this of our reason to faith takes not away the land-marks of knowledge. This shakes not the foundations of reason but leaves us that use of our faculties, for which they were given us.

INDEX.

Abstraction, abstract ideas, how formed, 106, 107; the meaning of such ideas, 108.
Assent, distinguished from knowledge, 141; degrees of, 144–147.
Association, nature of, 99; influence of, upon our judgments, 100.

Being, 136, 138.

Cause, origin of the idea, 85, 86.
Certainty, where found, 125; distinguished from probability, 132.
Comparison, 54.
Compounding, 55.

Duration, idea of, 63, 64; meaning of, 65; duration and time and space, 67, 69.

Essence, meaning of, 108, 109; real and nominal, 110 ff.; our knowledge of, 110 ff., 122, 123.
Eternity, idea of, how obtained, 66; our knowledge of, 72, 73; relation to time, 73.
Existence, idea of, 44; our knowledge of, 132 ff., 140, 141.
Extension, idea of, 60; relation to space, 60; relation to body, 61–63; distinguished from solidity, 62.
External objects, our knowledge of, 133, 140 ff.
Faith, faith and knowledge, 143; nature of, 153; relation to reason, 155 ff.; faith and revelation, 155 ff.

God, proofs of his existence, 133 ff.

Ideas, definition of, 32, 52; ideas not innate, 32 ff.; ideas from experience only, 35; simple ideas, 39 ff.; ideas of sensation and reflection, 36; ideas and qualities, 45, 46; primary and secondary ideas, 45 ff; complex ideas, 52 ff.; clear and obscure ideas, 94; real and fantastical ideas, 95; adequate and inadequate ideas, 96, 97; ideas and knowledge, 112, 113.
Identity, idea of, how formed, 86, 87; material identity, 87; identity of living being, 88 ff.; personal identity, 90 ff.
Inference, nature of, 151; inference and syllogism, 151.
Infinity, idea of, 70; negative and positive idea of, 70 ff.; infinity and space, 71, 72.

Judgment, definition of, 141; relation to knowledge, 142, 143; judgment and probability, 143 ff.

Knowledge, source of, 32, 35; knowledge and ideas, 112; nature of, 112, 113; degrees of, 115; intuitive knowledge, 115 ff.; demonstrative knowledge, 117; extent of knowledge, 118 ff.; sensitive knowledge, 126, 138; reality of knowledge, 129 ff.; knowledge of self, 134; of God,

159

133 ff.; of external object, 137 ff.

Language, 101, 102.

Matter, not first cause, 137, 138; matter and thought, 139.

Memory, nature of, 52; failure of, 53; aids to, 53.

Miracles, 146.

Modes and simple ideas, 58; simple and mixed modes, 58, 76; modes of space, 60; modes of thinking, 74 ff.

Names, use of, 103; meaning, 103 ff.; names of substances, 108, 109 ff.; names and essences, nominal and real, 109, 110 ff.

Nature, our knowledge of, 123, 124.

Number, 69–71.

Opinion, 143.

Perception, nature of, 42; ideas of, 50, 51; original and acquired, 50, 51.

Person, 91, 92; personal identity, 91 ff.; what makes personal identity, 91, 92.

Place, 60.

Power, our knowledge of, 44, 75; power and relation, 76; power and qualities of bodies, 76.

Probability, definition of, 143; grounds of, 143; degrees of, 146, 147.

Proposition, definition of, 114; verbal, trifling, and significant, 114, 131; true and false propositions, 123, 124.

Qualities and ideas, 45, 46; distinction of qualities, 46 ff.

Reason, office of, 47; reasoning and the syllogism, 150 ff; reason and faith, 153, 151; reason and revelation, 155.

Reflection, reflection a source of ideas, 35; defined, 36; ideas that are derived from reflection, 42 ff.

Relation, idea of, how obtained, 83, 84; forms of relation, 85, 86.

Retention, 52.

Revelation, its relation to reason, 145; as a source of knowledge, 154, 155; authority of, 156, 157.

Self, 93.

Sensation, a source of knowledge, 35.

Solidity, simple idea, 41; its relation to space, 42.

Soul, 35.

Space, the idea of, 60; modes of, 61.

Spirits, 146.

Substance, idea of, how formed, 58 ff.; substance in general, and particular substances, 79, 80; collective ideas of, 83; substance and personal identity, 92 ff.; corporeal and thinking substance, 120; our knowledge of substances, 120 ff.

Succession, idea of, 44; succession and duration, 62.

Syllogism, relation to reasoning, 152 ff.; objects of, 152 ff.

Thinking, 92, 93.

Time, 61, 62.

Truth, relation to knowledge, 114; kinds of, 114, 115.

Willing, 42.

Words, 101, 102.

www.ingramcontent.com/pod-product-compliance
Lightning Source LLC
Chambersburg PA
CBHW030253170426
43202CB00009B/721